THE

Queen-like CLOSET,

OR

Rich Cabinet.

1. *To make* Aqua Mirabilis *a very delicate way.*

Take three Pints of Sack, three Pints of White Wine, one quart of the Spirit of Wine, one quart of the juice of Celandine leaves, of Melilot-flowers, Cardamum-seeds, Cubebs, Galingale, Nutmegs, Cloves, Mace, Ginger, two Drams of each; bruise them, and mix them with the Wine and Spirits, let it stand all night in the Still, not an Alembeck, but a common Still, close stopped with Rye Paste; the next morning make a slow fire in the Still, and all the while it is stilling, keep a wet Cloth about the neck of the Still, and put so much white Sugar Candy as you think fit into the Glass where it drops.

2. *The Plague-Water which was most esteemed of in the late great Visitation.*

Take three Pints of Muskadine, boil therein one handful of Sage, and one handful of Rue until a Pint be wasted, then strain it out, and set it over the Fire again.

Put thereto a Penniworth of Long Pepper, half an Ounce of Ginger, and a quarter of an Ounce of Nutmegs, all beaten together, boil them together a little while close covered, then put to it one penniworth of Mithridate, two penniworth of Venice Treacle, one quarter of a Pint of hot Angelica Water.

Take one Spoonful at a time, morning and evening always warm, if you be already diseased; if not, once a day is sufficient all the Plague time.

It is most excellent Medicine, and never faileth, if taken before the heart be utterly mortified with the Disease, it is also good for the Small Pox, Measles, or Surfets.

3. *A very Soveraign Water.*

Take one Gallon of good Claret Wine, then take Ginger, Galingale, Cinnamon, Nutmegs, Grains, Cloves, Anniseeds, Fennel-seeds, Caraway-seeds, of each one dram; then take Sage, Mint, Red-Rose leaves, Thyme, Pellitory of the Wall, Rosemary, Wild Thyme, Camomile, Lavander, of each one handful, bruise the Spices small and beat the Herbs, and put them into the Wine, and so let stand twelve hours close covered, stirring it divers times, then still it in an Alembeck, and keep the best Water by it self, and so keep every Water by it self; the first you may use for aged People, the other for younger.

This most excellent Water was from Dr. *Chambers*, which he kept secret till he had done many Cures therewith; it comforteth the Vital Spirits; it helpeth the inward Diseases that come of Cold; the shaking of the Palsie; it helpeth the Conception of Women that are barren; it killeth the Worms within the Body, helpeth the Stone within the Bladder; it cureth the Cold, Cough, and Tooth-ach, and comforteth the Stomach; it cureth the Dropsie, and cleanseth the Reins; it helpeth speedily the stinking Breath; whosoever useth this Water, it preserveth them in good health, and maketh seem young very long; for it comforteth Nature very much; with this water Dr. *Chambers* preserved his own life till extreme Age would suffer him neither to go nor stand one whit, and he continued five years after all Physicians judged he could not live; and he confessed that when he was sick at any time, he never used any other Remedy but this Water, and wished his Friends when he lay upon his Deth-Bed to make use of it for the preservation of their Health.

4. *To Make Spirit of Mints.*

Take three Pints of the best white Wine, three handfuls of right Spear mint picked clean from the stalks, let it steep in the wine one night covered, in the morning, put it into a Copper Alembeck, and draw it with a pretty quick fire; and when you have drawn it all, take all your Water and add as much Wine as before, and put to the Water, and the same quantity of Mint as before; let it steep two or three hours, then put all into your Still, and draw it with a soft fire, put into your Receiver a quantity of Loaf Sugar, and you will find it very excellent; you may distil it in an ordinary Still if you please; but then it will not be so strong nor effectual.

Thus you may do with any other Herbs whatsoever.

5. *To make the Cordial Orange-Water.*

Take one dozen and a half of the highest coloured and thick rin'd Oranges, slice them thin, and put them into two Pints of Malago Sack, and one Pint of the best Brandy, of Cinamon, Nutmegs, Ginger, Cloves, and Mace, of each one quarter of an Ounce bruised, of Spear-mint and Balm one handful of each, put them into an ordinary Still all night, pasted up with Rye Paste; the next day draw them with a slow fire, and keep a wet Cloth upon the Neck of the Still; put in some Loaf Sugar into the Glass where it dropeth.

6. *To make Spirit of Oranges or of Limons.*

Take of the thickest rin'd Oranges or Limons, and chip off the Rinds very thin, put these Chips into a Glass-bottle, and put in as many as the Glass will hold, then put in as much Malago Sack as the Glass will hold besides; stop the bottle close that no Air get in, and when you use it, take about half a spoonful in a Glass of Sack; it is very good for the Wind in the Stomach.

7. *To make Limon Water.*

Take twelve of the fairest Limons, slice them, and put them into two Pints of white Wine, and put to them of Cinamon and Galingale, of each, one quarter of an Ounce, of Red Rose Leaves, Burrage and Bugloss Flowers, of each one handful, of yellow Sanders one Dram, steep all these together 12 hours, then distil them gently in a Glass Still, put into the Glass where it droppeth, three Ounces of Sugar, and one Grain of Amber-Greece.

8. *A Water for fainting of the Heart.*

Take of Bugloss water and Red Rose Water, of each one Pint, of Red Cows milk half a Pint, Anni-seed and Cinamon of each half an Ounce bruised, Maiden hair two handfuls, Harts-tongue one handful, bruise them, and mix all these together, and distil them in an ordinary Still, drink of it Morning and Evening with a little Sugar.

9. *To make Rosemary Water.*

Take a Quart of Sack or white Wine with as many Rosemary Flowers as will make it very thick, two Nutmegs, and two Races of Ginger sliced thin into it; let it infuse all night, then distil it in an ordinary Still as your other waters.

10. *To make a most precious Water.*

Take two Quarts of Brandy, of Balm, of Wood-Betony, of Pellitory of the Wall, of sweet Marjoram, of Cowslip-Flowers, Rosemary-Flowers, Sage-Flowers, Marigold-Flowers, of each of these one handful bruised together; then take one Ounce of Gromwell seeds, one Ounce of sweet Fennel seeds, one Ounce of Coriander seeds bruised, also half an Ounce of Aniseeds and half an Ounce of Caraway-seeds, half an Ounce of Juniper Berries, half an Ounce of Bay Berries, One Ounce of green Licoras, three Nutmegs, one quarter of an Ounce of large Mace, one quarter of an Ounce of Cinamon, one quarter of an Ounce of Cloves, half an Ounce of Ginger, bruise all these well together, then add to them half a pound of Raisons in the Sun stoned, let all these steep together in the Brandy nine days close stopped, then strain it out, and two Grains of Musk, two of Amber-Greece, one pound of refined Sugar; stop the Glass that no Air get in, and keep it in a warm place.

11. *Doctor* Butler's *Treacle Water.*

Take the roots of Polipody of the Oak bruised, *Lignum Vitæ* thin sliced, the inward part thereof, Saxifrage roots thin sliced, of the shavings of Hartshorn, of each half a pound, of the outward part of yellow Citron not preserved; one Ounce and half bruised, mix these together;

Then take

   {Fumitory water}
  {Carduus-water } Of each one
of {Camomile-water} Ounce.
   {Succory-water }

of Cedar wood one Ounce, of Cinamon three drams, of Cloves three drams, bruise all your forenamed things;

Then take of Epithimum two ounces and a half, of Cerratch six ounces, of Carduus and Balm, of each two handfuls, of Burrage Flowers, Bugloss Flowers, Gillyflowers, of each four ounces, of Angelica root, Elecampane root beaten to a Pap, of each four ounces, of Andronichus Treacle and Mithridate, of each four ounces; mix all these together, and incorporate them well, and grind them in a Stone Mortar, with part of the former Liquor, and at last, mix all together, and let them stand warm 24 hours close stopped, then put them all into a Glass Still, and sprinkle on the top of *Species Aromatica rosata* and *Diambre*, of the Species of *Diarodon abbatis*, *Diatrion Santalon*, of each six drams; then cover the Still close, and lute it well, and distill the water with a soft fire, and keep it close.

This will yield five Pints of the best water, the rest will be smaller.

12. *The Cordial Cherry Water.*

Take nine pounds of red Cherries, nine pints of Claret Wine, eight ounces of Cinamon, three ounces of Nutmegs; bruise your Spice, stone your Cherries, and steep them in the Wine, then add to them half a handful of Rosemary, half a handful of Balm, one quarter of a handful of sweet Marjoram, let them steep in an earthen Pot twenty four hours, and as you put them into the Alembeck, to distil them, bruise them with your hands, and make a soft fire under them, and distil by degrees; you may mix the waters at your pleasure when you have drawn them all; when you have thus done, sweeten it with Loaf-Sugar, then strain it into another Glass, and stop it close that no Spirits go out; you may (if you please) hang a Bag with Musk and Amber-greece in it, when you use it, mix it with Syrrup of Gilly-flowers or of Violets, as you best like it; it is an excellent Cordial for Fainting fits, or a Woman in travel, or for any one who is not well.

13. *A most excellent Water for the Stone, or for the Wind-Cholick.*

Take two handfuls of Mead-Parsly, otherwise called Saxifrage, one handful of Mother-Thyme, two handfuls of Perstons, two handfuls of Philipendula, and as much Pellitory of the Wall, two ounces of sweet Fennel seeds, the roots of ten Radishes sliced, steep all these in a Gallon of Milk warm from the Cow, then distil it in an ordinary Still, and four hours after, slice half an ounce of the wood called Saxifrage, and put into the Bottle to the water, keep it close stopped, and take three spoonfuls at a time, and fast both from eating and drinking one hour after; you must make this water about Midsummer; it is a very precious water, and ought to be prized.

14. *The Cock water, most delicate and precious for restoring out of deep Consumptions, and for preventing them, and for curing of Agues, proved by my self and many others.*

Take a Red Cock, pluck him alive, then slit him down the back, and take out his Intrals, cut him in quarters, and bruise him in a Mortar, with his Head, Legs, Heart, Liver and Gizard; put him into an ordinary Still with a Pottle of Sack, and one quart of Milk new from a red Cow, one pound of blew Currants beaten, one pound of Raisins in the Sun stoned and beaten, four Ounces of Dates stoned and beaten, two handfuls of Peniroyal, two handfuls of Pimpernel, or any other cooling Herb, one handful of Mother-thyme, one handful of Rosemary one handful of Burrage, one quart of Red Rose water, two ounces of Harts-horn, two ounces of China root sliced, two ounces of Ivory shaving, four ounces of the flower of French Barley; put all these into your Still and paste it up very well, and still it with a soft fire, put into the Glass where it droppeth one pound of white Sugar Candy beaten very small, twelve peniworth of Leaf-Gold, seven grains of Musk, eleven grains of Amber-greece, seven grains of Bezoar stone; when it is all distilled, mix all the waters together, and every morning fasting, and every evening when you go to bed, take four or five Spoonfuls of it warm, for about a Month together, this hath cured many when the Doctors have given them over.

15. *Walnut water, or the Water of Life.*

Take green Walnuts in the beginning of *June*, beat them in a Mortar, and distil them in an ordinary Still, keep that Water by it self, then about Midsummer gather some more, and distil them as you did before, keep that also by it self, then take a quart of each and mix them together, and distil them in a Glass Still, and keep it for your use; the Virtues are as followeth; It will help all manner of Dropsies and Palsies, drank with Wine fasting; it is good for the eyes, if you put one drop therein; it helpeth Conception in Women if they drink thereof one spoonful at a time in a Glass of Wine once a day, and it will make your skin fair if you wash therewith; it is good for all infirmities of the Body, and driveth out all Corruption, and inward Bruises; if it be drunk with Wine moderately, it killeth Worms in the Body; whosoever drinketh much of it, shall live so long as Nature shall continue in him.

Finally, if you have any Wine that is turned, put in a little Viol or Glass full of it, and keep it close stopped, and within four days it will come to it self again.

16. *To make Wormwood Water.*

Take four ounces of Aniseeds, four ounces of Licoras scraped, bruise them well with two ounces of Nutmegs, add to them one good handful of Wormwood, one root of Angelica, steep them in three Gallons of Sack Lees and strong Ale together twelve hours; then distill them in an Alembeck, and keep it for your use.

17. *A very rare Cordial Water.*

Take one Gallon of white Wine, two ounces of Mithridate, two ounces of Cinamon, one handful of Balm, a large handful of Cowslips, two handfuls of Rosemary Flowers, half an ounce of Mace, half an ounce of Cloves, half an ounce of Nutmegs, all bruised, steep these together four days in an earthen Pot, and covered very close, distil them in an ordinary Still well pasted, and do it with a very slow fire; save the first water by it self, and the small by it self, to give to Children; when you have occasion to use it, take a spoonful thereof, sweetned with Loaf-Sugar; this Water is good to drive out any Infection from the heart, and to comfort the Spirits.

18. *Another most excellent Cordial.*

Take Celandine, Sage, Costmary, Rue, Wormwood, Mugwort, Scordium, Pimpernel, Scabious, Egrimony, Betony, Balm, Carduus, Centory, Peniroyal, Elecampane roots, Tormentil with the roots, Horehound, Rosa Solis, Marigold Flowers, Angelica, Dragon, Marjoram, Thyme, Camomile, of each two good handfuls; Licoras, Zedoary, of each one ounce; slice the Roots, shred the Herbs, and steep them in four quarts of white Wine, and let it stand close covered 2 days, then distil it in an ordinary Still pasted up; when you use it, sweeten it with fine Sugar, and warm it.

19. *To make* Rosa Solis.

Take a Pottle of *Aqua Composita*, and put it into a Glass, then a good handful of *Rosa Solis* clean picked, but not washed, put it to the *Aqua Composita*, then take a pound of Dates stoned and beaten small, half a peniworth of Long Pepper, as much of Grains, and of round Pepper, bruise them small, take also a pound of Loaf-Sugar well beaten, a quarter of a pound of Powder of Pearl, and six leaves of Book Gold; put all to the rest, and stir them well together in the Glass, then cover it very close, and let it stand in the Sun fourteen days, ever taking it in at night; then strain it, and put it into a close Bottle; you must not put in the Pearl, Gold or Sugar till it hath been sunned and strained, neither must you touch the Leaves of the *Rosa Solis* with your hands when you pick it; keep it very close.

20. *The Heart Water.*

Take five handfuls of Rosemary Flowers, two drams of red Coral, two drams of Powder of Pearl, two drams of white Amber, two drams of Cinamon, two pound of the best Prunes stoned, six Pints of Damask Rose water, two Pints of Sack; put all these into a Pipkin never used, stop it up with Paste, let them stand upon a soft fire a little while, then distil it in an ordinary Still pasted up.

21. *The Plague Water.*

Take Rosemary, Red Balm, Burrage, Angelica, Carduus, Celandine, Dragon, Featherfew, Wormwood, Penyroyal, Elecampane roots, Mugwort, Bural, Tormentil, Egrimony, Sage, Sorrel, of each of these one handful, weighed weight for weight; put all these in an earthen Pot, with four quarts of white Wine, cover them close, and let them stand eight or nine days in a cool Cellar, then distil it in a Glass Still.

22. *The Treacle Water.*

Take one pound of old Venice Treacle, of the Roots of Elecampane, Gentian, Cyprus, Tormentil, of each one ounce, of Carduus and Angelica, half an ounce, of Burrage, Bugloss, and of Rosemary Flowers one ounce of each; infuse these in three Pints of white Wine, one Pint of Spring Water, two Pints of Red Rose water; then distil them in an ordinary Still pasted up.

This is excellent for Swounding Fits or Convulsions, and expelleth any venomous Disease; it also cureth any sort of Agues.

23. *The Snail water excellent for Consumptions.*

Take a Peck of Snails with the Shells on their Backs, have in a readiness a good fire of Charcoal well kindled, make a hole in the midst of the fire, and cast your Snails into the fire, renew your fire till the Snails are well rosted, then rub them with a clean Cloth, till you have rubbed off all the green which will come off.

Then bruise them in a Mortar, shells and all, then take Clary, Celandine, Burrage, Scabious, Bugloss, five leav'd Grass, and if you find your self hot, put in some Wood-Sorrel, of every one of these one handful, with five tops of Angelica.

These Herbs being all bruised in a Mortar, put them in a sweet earthen Pot with five quarts of white Wine, and two quarts of Ale, steep them all night; then put them into an Alembeck, let the herbs be in the bottom of the Pot, and the Snails upon the Herbs, and upon the Snails put a Pint of Earth-worms slit and clean washed in white Wine, and put upon them four ounces of Anniseeds or Fennel-seeds well bruised, and five great handfuls of Rosemary Flowers well picked, two or three Races of Turmerick thin sliced, Harts-horn and Ivory, of each four ounces, well steeped in a quart of white Wine till it be like a Jelly, then draw it forth with care.

24. *To make a rare sweet Water.*

Take sweet Marjoram, Lavender, Rosemary, Muscovy, Maudlin, Balm, Thyme, Walnut Leaves, Damask Roses, Pinks, of all a like quantity, enough to fill your Still, then take of the best Orrice Powder, Damask Rose Powder, and Storax, of each two ounces; strew one handful or two of your Powders upon the Herbs, then distil them with a soft fire; tie a little Musk in a piece of Lawn, and hang it in the Glass wherein it drops, and when it is all drawn out, take your sweet Cakes and mix them with the Powders which are left, and lay among your Clothes, or with sweet Oyles, and burn them for perfume.

25. *A very good Surfet water.*

Take what quantity of Brandy you please, steep a good quantity of the Flowers of Red Poppies therein, which grow amongst the Wheat, having the black bottoms cut off, when they have been steeped long enough, strain them out, and put in new, and so do till the Brandy be very red with them, and let it stand in the Sun all the while they infuse, then put in Nutmegs, Cloves, Ginger and Cinamon, with some fine Sugar, so much as you think fit, and keep it close stopped; this is very good for Surfets, Wind in the Stomach, or any Illness whatever.

26. *An excellent Water for the Stomach, or against Infection.*

Take Carduus, Mint and Wormwood, of each a like quantity, shred them small and put them into new Milk, distil them in an ordinary Still with a temperate fire; when you take any of it, sweeten it with Sugar, or with any Syrrup, what pleases you best; it is a very good water, though the Ingredients are but mean.

27. *The Melancholy Water.*

Take of the Flowers of Gilliflowers, four handfuls, Rosemary flowers three handfuls, Damask Rose leaves, Burrage and Bugloss flowers of each one handful, of Balm leaves six handfuls, of Marigold flowers one handful, of Pinks six handfuls, of Cinamon grosly beaten, half an ounce, two Nutmegs beaten, Anniseeds beaten one ounce, three peniworth of Saffron; put them all into a Pottle of Sack, and let them stand two days, stirring them sometimes well together; then distil them in an ordinary Still, and let it drop into a Glass wherein there is two grains of Musk, and eight ounces of white Sugar Candy, and some Leaf-Gold; take of this Water three times a week fasting, two spoonfuls at a time, and ofter if you find need; distil with soft fire; this is good for Women in Child-bed if they are faint.

28. *To make the Elder water, or spirit of* Sambucus.

Take some Rye Leaven, and break it small into some warm Water, let it be a sowre one, for that is best; about two Ounces or more: then take a Bushel of Elder Berries beaten small, and put them into an earthen Pot and mix them very well with the Leaven, and let it stand one day near the Fire; then put in a little Yest, and stir it well together to make it rise, so let it stand ten days covered, and sometimes stir it; then distil it in an Alembeck; keep the first Water by it self, and so the second, and the third will be good Vinegar, if afterward you colour it with some of the Berries.

Distil it with a slow fire, and do not fill the Still too full.

This Water is excellent for the Stomach.

29. *To make the Balm water Green.*

Take any Wine or Lees of Wine, or good Strong Beer or Ale with the Grounds, and stir them all together very well, lest the Wine Lees be too thick, and burn the bottom of the Pot; put them into an Alembeck with good store of Balm unwashed, therein still these till you leave no other tast but fair water, and draw also some of that, draw two Alembecks full more as you draw the first, until you have so much as will fill your Alembeck, then put this distilled water into your Alembeck again, and some more Balm, if you draw a Wine Gallon, put to it half a pound of Coriander seeds bruised, two Ounces of Cloves, one quarter of an Ounce of Nutmegs, and one quarter of an Ounce of Mace bruised all of them, then set a Receiver of a Gallon under it, and fill it with fresh and green Balm unwashed, and your Water will be as green as Grass; put still more and more of the Herbs fresh, and let it stand a week to make it the more green.

Take this Green Water, and put to it one quart of the best Damask Rosewater, and before you mix your Balm-water and Rose-water together, you must dissolve two pounds of fine Sugar in the first distilled water, then take Ambergreece and Musk, of each eight Grains, being ground fine, and put it into the Glass in a piece of Lawn; put also a little Orange or Limon Pill to it, and keep it cool and from the Air.

30. *To make the very best Surfet-water.*

Take one Gallon of the best French Spirits, and a Pint of Damask-Rose-water, half a Pint of Poppy water, one pound of white Sugar Candy bruised, then take one pound and half of Raisins in the Sun stoned, half a pound of Dates stoned and sliced, then take one Ounce of Mace, one Ounce of Cloves, one Ounce of Cinamon, one Ounce of Aniseeds rubbed clean from the dust, then take a quarter of an Ounce of Licoras clean scraped and sliced, and all the Spices grosly beaten, let all these steep in the Spirits four days; then take a quarter of a peck of Red Poppy Leaves fresh gathered, and the black part cut off, and put them in, and when it hath stood four or five days, strain it, and put it into your Glass, then put in your Sugar-Candy finely beaten, twelve peniworth of Ambergreece, six peniworth of Musk, keep it close, and shake it now and then, and when you use it, you may put some kind of Syrrup to it, what you please.

31. *To make the true Palsie-water, as it was given by that once very famous Physician Doctor* Matthias.

Take Lavender Flowers stripped from the stalks, and fill a Gallon-Glass with them, and pour on them good Spirit of Sack, or perfect *Aqua vitæ* distilled from all Flegm, let the quantity be five quarts, then circulate them for six weeks, very close with a Bladder, that nothing may breath out; let them stand in a warm place, then distil them in an Alembeck with his Cooler, then put into the said water, of Sage, Rosemary, and Wood-Betony Flowers; of each half a handful, of Lilly of the Valley, and Burrage, Bugloss, and Cowslip Flowers, one handful of each; steep these in Spirit of Wine, Malmsie, or *Aqua vitæ*, every one in their Season, till all may be had; then put also to them of Balm, Motherwort, Spike-flowers, Bay leaves, the leaves of Orange trees, with the Flowers, if they may be had, of each one ounce, put them into the aforesaid distilled Wine all together, and distil it as before, having first been steeped six weeks; when you have distilled it, put into it Citron Pill, dried Piony seeds hull'd, of each five Drams, of Cinamon half an Ounce, of Nutmegs, Cardamum seeds, Cubebs, and yellow Saunders, of each half an ounce, of lignum Aloes one dram; make all these into Powder, and put them into the distilled Wine abovesaid, and put to them of Cubebs anew, a good half pound of Dates, the stones taken out, and cut them in small pieces, put all these in, and close your Vessel well with a double Bladder; let them digest six weeks, then strain it hard with a Press, and filtrate the Liquor, then put into it of prepared Pearl, Smaragdus, Musk and Saffron, of each half a Scruple; and of Ambergreece one Scruple, red Roses dried well, Red and Yellow Saunders, of each one ounce, hang these in a Sarsenet Bag in the water, being well sewed that nothing go out.

The virtues of this Water.

This Water is of exceeding virtue in all Swoundings and Weaknesses of the heart, and decaying of Spirits in all Apoplexies and Palsies, also in all pains of the Joints coming of Cold, for all Bruises outwardly bathed and dipped Clothes laid to; it strengtheneth and comforteth all animal, natural and viral Spirits, and cheareth the external Senses, strengtheneth the Memory, restoreth lost Speech, and lost Appetite, all weakness of the Stomach, being both taken inwardly, and bathed outwardly; it taketh away the Giddiness of the Head, helpeth lost Hearing, it maketh a pleasant

Breath, helpeth all cold disposition of the Liver, and a beginning Dropsie; it helpeth all cold Diseases of the Mother; indeed none can express sufficiently; it is to be taken morning and evening, about half a Spoonful with Crums of Bread and Sugar.

32. *For a Cough of the Lungs, or any Cough coming of Cold, approved by many.*

Take a good handful of French Barley, boil it in several waters till you see the water be clear, then take a quart of the last water, and boil in it sliced Licoras, Aniseeds bruised, of each as much as you can take up with your four Fingers and your Thumb, Violet Leaves, Strawberry Leaves, five fingered Grass, Maidenhair, of each half a handful, a few Raisins in the Sun stoned; boil these together till it come to a Pint, then strain it, and take twelve or fourteen Jordan Almonds blanched and beaten, and when your water is almost cold, put in your Almonds, and stir it together, and strain it; then sweeten it with white Sugar Candy; drink this at four times, in the morning fasting, and at four of the Clock in the Afternoon a little warmed; do this nine or ten days together; if you please, you may take a third draught when you go to Bed; if you be bound in your body, put in a little Syrrup of Violets, the best way to take it, is to suck it through a straw, for that conveys it to the Lungs the better.

33. *To make the best Bisket-Cakes.*

Take four new laid Eggs, leave out two of the Whites, beat them very well, then put in two spoonfuls of Rose-water, and, beat them very well together, then put in a pound of double refin'd Sugar beaten and searced, and beat them together one hour, then put to them one pound of fine Flower, and still beat them together a good while; then put them upon Plates rubbed over with Butter, and set them into the Oven as fast as you can, and have care you do not bake them too much.

34. *Perfumed Roses.*

Take Damask Rose Buds, and cut off the Whites, then take Rose-water or Orange-Flower water wherein hath been steeped *Benjamin, Storax, Lignum Rhodium,* Civet or Musk, dip some Cloves therein and stick into every Bud one, you must stick them in where you cut away the Whites; dry them between white Papers, they will then fall asunder; this Perfume will last seven years.

Or do thus.

Take your Rose Leaves cut from the Whites, and sprinkle them with the aforesaid water, and put a little powder of Cloves among them.

35. *To make Tincture of Caraways.*

Take one quart of the Spirits of French Wine, put into it one pound of Caraway Comfits which are purled, and the Pills of two Citron Limons; let it stand in a warm place to infuse, in a Glass close stopped for a Month, stirring it every day once.

Then strain it from the seeds, and add to it as much Rosewater as will make it of a pleasant taste, then hang in your Bottle a little Ambergreece, and put in some Leaf-Gold; this is a very fine Cordial.

36. *To get away the Signs of the Small Pox.*

Quench some Lime in white Rosewater, then shake it very well, and use it at your pleasure; when you at any time have washed with it, anoint your face with Pomatum, made with Spermaceti and oyl of sweet Almonds.

37. *To make clouted Cream.*

Take Milk that was milked in the morning, and scald it at noon; it must have a reasonable fire under it, but not too rash, and when it is scalding hot, that you see little Pimples begin to rise, take away the greatest part of the Fire, then let it stand and harden a little while, then take it off, and let it stand until the next day, covered, then take it off with a Skimmer.

38. *To make a* Devonshire-*White-pot.*

Take two quarts of new Milk, a peny white Loaf sliced very thin, then make the Milk scalding hot, then put to it the Bread, and break it, and strain it through a Cullender, then put in four Eggs, a little Spice, Sugar, Raisins, and Currans, and a little Salt, and so bake it, but not too much, for then it will whey.

39. *To make the* Portugal *Eggs.*

Take a very large Dish with a broad brim, lay in it some *Naples* Bisket in the Form of a Star, then put so much Sack into the Dish as you do think the Biskets will drink up; then stick them full with thin little pieces of preserved Orange, and green Citron Pill, and strew store of French Comfits over them, of divers colours, then butter some Eggs, and lay them here and there upon the Biskets, then fill up the hollow places in the Dish, with several coloured Jellies, and round about the Brim thereof lay Lawrel Leaves guilded with

Leaf-Gold; lay them flaunting, and between the Leaves several coloured Jellies.

40. *To Candy Flowers the best way.*

Takes Roses, Violets, Cowslips, or Gilly-flowers, and pick them from the white bottoms, then have boiled to a Candy height Sugar, and put in so many Flowers as the Sugar will receive, and continually stir them with the back of a Spoon, and when you see the Sugar harden on the sides of the Skillet, and on the Spoon, take them off the Fire, and keep them with stirring in the warm Skillet, till you see them part, and the Sugar as it were sifted upon them, then put them upon a paper while they are warm and rub them gently with your hands; till all the Lumps be broken, then put them into a Cullender, and sift them as clean as may be, then pour them upon a clean Cloth, and shake them up and down till there be hardly any Sugar hanging about them; then if you would have them look as though they were new gathered, have some help, and open them with your fingers before they be quite cold, and if any Sugar hang about them, you may wipe it off with a fine Cloth; to candy Rosemary Flowers, or Archangel, you must pull out the string that stands up in the middle of the Blossom, and take them which are not at all faded, and they will look as though they were new gathered, without opening.

41. *To pickle Cucumbers.*

Take the least you can get, and lay a layer of Cucumbers, and then a layer of beaten Spices, Dill, and Bay Leaves, and so do till you have filled your Pot, and let the Spices, Dill, and Bay Leaves cover them, then fill up your Pot with the best Wine Vinegar, and a little Salt, and so keep them.

Sliced Turneps also very thin, in some Vinegar, Pepper and a little Salt, do make a very good Sallad, but they will keep but six Weeks.

42. *To make Sugar Cakes.*

Take a pound of fine Sugar beaten and searced, with four Ounces of the finest Flower, put to it one pound of Butter well washed with Rose-water, and work them well together, then take the Yolks of four Eggs, and beat them with four Spoonfuls of Rosewater, in which hath been steeped two or three days before Nutmeg and Cinamon, then put thereto so much Cream as will make it knead to a stiff Paste, rowl it into thin Cakes, and prick them, and lay them on Plates, and bake them; you shall not need to butter your Plates, for they will slip off of themselves, when they are cold.

43. *To make a very fine Cream.*

Take a quart of Cream, and put to it some Rosewater and Sugar, some large Mace, Cinamon and Cloves; boil it together for a quarter of an hour, then take the yolks of eight Eggs, beat them together with some of your Cream, then put them into the Cream which is boiling, keep it stirring lest it curdle, take it from the fire, and keep it stirring till it be a little cold, then run it through a Strainer, dish it up, and let it stand one night, the next day it will be as stiff as a Custard, then stick it with blanched Almonds, Citron Pill and Eringo roots, and so serve it in.

44. *To make Syrup of Turneps for a Consumption.*

Take half a peck of Turneps washed and pared clean, cut them thin, put to them one pound of Raisins of the Sun stoned, one quarter of a pound of Figs cut small, one Ounce of Anniseeds bruised, half an Ounce of Licoras sliced, one Ounce of Cloves bruised, two handfuls of Burrage Flowers, and so much water as will cover all, and two fingers breadth above them, then boil it on a great fire in an earthen Vessel covered, untill the roots be soft and tender, then strain out the Liquor, and to every Pint of it put a pound of fine Sugar, the whites of two Eggs beaten, boil it to a Syrrop, and use it often, two or three spoonfuls at a time.

45. *For a Consumption.*

Take a Pint of Red Cows milk, then take the Yolk of a new laid Egg potched very rare, then stir it into the Milk over a soft fire, but do not let it boil, sweeten it with a little Sugar Candy, and drink it in the morning fasting, and when you go to bed.

46. *To make Bottle Ale for a Consumption.*

Take a quart of Ale, and a Pint of strong *Aqua vitæ*, Mace and Cinamon, of each one quarter of an Ounce, two Spoonfuls of the powder Elecampane root, one quarter of a pound of Loaf Sugar, one quarter of a pound of Raisins of the Sun stoned, four spoonfuls of Aniseeds beaten to Powder, then put all together into a Bottle and stop it close.

Take three spoonfuls of this in a morning fasting, and again one hour before Supper and shake the Bottle when you pour it out.

47. *To make Cakes of Quinces.*

Take the best you can get, and pare them, and slice them thin from the Core, then put them into a Gallipot close stopped, and tie it down with a Cloth, and put it into a Kettle of boiling water, so that it may stand steddy about five hours, and as your water boils away in the Kettle, fill it up with more warm water, then pour your Quinces into a fine hair sieve, and let it drain all the Liquor into a Bason, then take this Liquor and weigh it, and to every pound take a pound of double refin'd Sugar, boil this Sugar to a Candy height, then put in your Liquor, and set them over a slow fire, and stir them continually till you see it will Jelly, but do not let it boil; then put it into Glasses, and set them in a Stove till you see them with a Candy on the top, then turn them out with a wet Knife on the other side upon a white Paper, sleeked over with a sleek-stone, and set them in the Stove again till the other side be dry, and then keep them in a dry place.

48. *To make Marmalade of Apricocks.*

Take Apricocks, pare them and cut them in quarters, and to every pound of Apricocks put a pound of fine Sugar, then put your Apricocks into a Skillet with half of the Sugar, and let them boil very tender and gently, and bruise them with the back of a Spoon, till they be like Pap, then take the other part of the Sugar, and boil it to a Candy height, then put your Apricocks into that Sugar, and keep it stirring over the fire, till all the Sugar be melted, but do not let it boil, then take it from the fire, and stir it till it be almost cold; then put it in Glasses, and let it have the Air of the fire to dry it.

49. *To make Limon Cakes.*

Take half a pound of refin'd sugar, put to it two spoonfuls of Rosewater, as much Orange Flower water, and as much of fair water, boil it to a Candy height, then put in the Rind of a Limon grated, and a little Juice, stir it well on the fire, and drop it on Plates or sleeked Paper.

50. *To make Wafers.*

Take a quart of Flower heaped and put to it the yolks of four Eggs, and two or three spoonfuls of Rosewater, mingle this well together, then make it like Batter with Cream and a little Sugar, and bake it on Irons very thin poured on.

51. *To make Marmalade of Cherries with Currans.*

Take four pounds of Cherries when they are stoned, and boil them alone in their Liquor for half an hour very fast, then pour away the Liquor from them, and put to them half a Pint and little more of the juice of Currans, then boil a pound of double refin'd Sugar to a Candy height, and put your Cherries and Juice of Currans in that, and boil them again very fast till you find it to jelly very well.

52. *To preserve Rasberries.*

Take the weight of your Rasberries in fine Sugar, and take some Rasberries and bruise them a little; then take the clearest of the bruised Rasberries, I mean the Juice and the weight of it in Sugar, and your other Sugar named before, and boil it, and scum it, then put in your whole Rasberries, and boil them up once, then let them stand over the fire without boiling till you see it will Jelly, and that it look clear, then take up your Rasberries one by one, and put them into Glasses, then boil your Syrrop, and put it over them.

53. *To make Syrrop of Ale, good for weak People to take inwardly, or to heal old Sores, applied thereto.*

Take two Gallons of Ale Wort, the strongest you can get, so soon as it is run from the Grounds, set it on the fire in a Pipkin, and let it boil gently and that you do perceive it to be as though it were full of Rags; run it through a strainer, and set it on the fire again, and let it boil until it be thick, and scum it clean, and when it is much wasted, put it into a lesser Pan to boil, or else it will burn; when it is thick enough, take it off, and when it is cold, put it into Gallipots, take as much as a Walnut fasting; and as much when you go to bed.

54. *To make whipt Sillibub.*

Take half a Pint of Rhenish Wine or white Wine, put it into a Pint of Cream, with the Whites of three Eggs, season it with Sugar, and beat it as you do Snow-Cream, with Birchen Rods, and take off the Froth as it ariseth, and put it into your Pot, so do till it be beaten to a Froth, let it stand two or three hours till it do settle, and then it will eat finely.

55. *To make Raisin Wine or Stepony.*

Take four Gallons of Spring-water, four pounds of Raisins of the Sun stoned, the juice of four good Limons, and the Rind of two cut thin, boil the Raisins, and Pill in the Water for half an hour or more, then put in the juice of Limon, and a little Spice, Sugar and Rosewater, and let it stand but a little more over the fire; then put it into an earthen pot, and beat it together till it be cold, then bottle it up, it will keep but a few days.

Memorandum, Two pounds of Sugar to one pound of Cowslips is enough for Conserve.

56. *To boil Samphire.*

Take Water and Salt so strong as will bear an Egg, boil it, and when it boils, put in your Samphire unwashed, and let it scald a little, then take it off, and cover it so close that no Air can get in, and set the Pot upon a cold Wisp of Hay, and so let it stand all night, and it will be very green, then put it up for your use.

57. *To make Cabbage Cream.*

Take twenty five Quarts of new Milk, set it on the fire till it be ready to boil, stir it all the while that it creams not, then pour it into twenty several Platters so fast as you can, when it is cold, take off the Cream with a Skimmer, and lay it on a Pie Plate in the fashion of a Cabbage, crumpled one upon another, do thus three times, and between every Layer you must mingle Rosewater and Sugar mingled thick, and laid on with a Feather; some use to take a little Cream and boil it with Ginger, then take it from the fire and season it with Rosewater and Sugar, and the Juice of Jordan Almonds blanched and beaten, then stir it till it be cold, that it cream not; then take Toasts of Manchet cut thin, not too hard, nor brown, lay them in the bottom of the Dish, and pour the Cream upon them, and lay the Cabbage over.

58. *To make a Trifle.*

Take sweet Cream, season it with Rosewater and Sugar, and a little whole Mace, let it boil a while, then take it off, and let it cool, and when it is lukewarm put it into such little Dishes or Bowls as you mean to serve it in; then put in a little Runnet, and stir it together; when you serve it in, strew on some French Comfits.

59. *To make thick Cream.*

Take sweet Cream, a little Flower finely searced, large Mace, a stick of Cinamon, Sugar and Rosewater, let all these boil together till it be thick, then put into it thick Cream, the yolks of Eggs beaten, then let it seeth but a little while for fear of turning, then pour it out, and when it is cold serve it in.

60. *To pickle Purslan to keep all the Year.*

Take the Leaves from the stalks, then take the Pot you mean to keep them in, and strew Salt over the bottom, then lay in a good row of the Leaves, and strew on more Salt, then lay in a row of the stalks, and put in more Salt, then a row of the Leaves, so keep it close covered.

61. *To Stretch Sheeps Guts.*

After they are clean scowred, lay them in water nine days, shifting them once a day, and they will be very easie to fill, and when they are filled, they will come to their wonted bigness.

62. *To make Cream of Pastes and Jellies.*

Put Eggs into the Cream as you do for Fool, and slice your Sweet-meats very thin and boil with them, then sweeten it, and put it into a Dish.

63. *To make a rare Medicine for the Chine-Cough.*

Make a Syrrop of Hysop-water and white Sugar Candy, then take the Powder of Gum Dragon, and as much of white Sugar Candy mixed together, and eat of it several times of the day, or take the above-named Syrrop, either of them will do the Cure.

64. *For a Consumption.*

Take of Syrrop of Violets, Syrrop of Horehound, Syrrop of Maidenhair and Conserve of Fox Lungs, of each one ounce, mix them well together, and take it often upon a Liquoras stick in the day time, and at night.

65. *To make very rare Ale.*

When your Ale is tunned into a Vessel that will hold eight or nine Gallons, and that hath done working, ready to be stopped up, then take a Pound and half of Raisins of the Sun stoned and cut in pieces, and two great Oranges, Meat and Rind, and sliced thin, with the Rind of one Limon, and a few Cloves, one Ounce of Coriander seeds bruised, put all these in a Bag, and hang them in the Vessel, and stop it up close; when it hath stood four days, bottle it up, fill the Bottles but a little above the Neck, and put into every one a Lump of fine Sugar, and stop them close, and let it be three Weeks or a month before you drink it.

66. *To make Ale to drink within a Week.*

Tun it into a Vessel which will hold eight Gallons, and when it hath done working, ready to bottle, put in some Ginger sliced, and an Orange stuck with Cloves, and cut here and there with a Knife, and a pound and half of Sugar, and with a stick stir it well together, and it will work afresh; when it hath done working, stop it close, and let it stand till it be clear, then bottle it up and put a Lump of Sugar into every Bottle, and then stop it close, and knock down the Corks, and turn the Bottles the Bottoms upwards, and it will be fit to drink in a Weeks time.

67. *For the Griping in the Guts.*

Take a peniworth of Brandy, and a peniworth of Mithridate mixed together, and drink it three nights together when you go to rest, or take a little Oil of Aniseeds in a Glass of Sack three times.

68. *To make a Sack Posset.*

Take twelve Eggs beaten very well, and put to them a Pint of Sack, stir them well that they curd not, then put to them three Pints of Cream, half a Pound of white Sugar, stirring them well together, when they are hot over the fire, put them into a Bason, and set the Bason over a boiling pot of water, until the Posset be like a Custard, then take it off, and when it is cool enough to eat, serve it in with beaten Spice strewed over it very thick.

69. *To make Pennado.*

Take Oatmeal clean picked and well beaten, steep it in water all night, then strain it and boil it in a Pipkin with some Currans, and a Blade or two of Mace, and a little Salt; when it is well boiled, take it off, and put in the Yolks of two or three new laid Eggs beaten with Rosewater, then set it on a soft fire, and stir it that it curd not, then sweeten it with Sugar, and put in a little Nutmeg.

70. *To make Cakes without Fruit.*

Take four pounds of fine Flower, rub into it one pound of Butter very well, then take warmed Cream, and temper it with Ale yest, so mix them together, and make them into a Paste, put in a little Rosewater, and several Spices well beaten, let it lie by the fire till the Oven heat, and when you make it up, knead into it half a pound of Caraway Comfits, and three quarters of a pound of Bisket-Comfits, make it up as fast as you can, not too thick, nor cut it too deep, put it into a hoop well butter'd, and wash it over with the White of an Egg, Rosewater, and Sugar, and strew it with some Comfits; do not bake it too much.

71. *A Sack Posset without Milk.*

Take thirteen Eggs and beat them very well, and while they are beating, take a quart of Sack, half a pound of fine Sugar, and a Pint of Ale, and let them boil a very little while, then put these Eggs to them, and stir them till they be hot, then take it from the fire, and keep it stirring a while, then put it into a fit Bason, and cover it close with a Dish, then set it over the fire again till it arise to a Curd; then serve it in with some beaten spice.

72. *A very fine Cordial.*

One Ounce of Syrrop of Gilly-flowers, one dram of Confection of Alkermes, one Ounce and a half of Burrage-water, the like of Mint-water, one Ounce of Dr. *Mountsford's* water, as much of Cinamon water mixed together.

73. *The best way to preserve Goosberries green and whole.*

Pick them clean and put them into water as warm as milk, so let them stand close covered half an hour, then put them into another warm water and let them stand as long, and so the third time, till you find them very green; then take their weight in fine Sugar, and make a Syrrop, then put them in, and let them boil softly one hour; then set them by till the next day, then heat them again, so do twice, then take them from that Syrrop and

92. *To make Almond Ginger-Bread.*

Take a little Gum-Dragon and lay it in steep in Rosewater all night, then take half a Pound of Jordan Almonds blanched and beaten with some of that Rosewater, then take half a pound of fine Sugar beaten and searced, of Ginger and Cinamon finely searced, so much as by your taste you may judge to be fit; beat all these together into a Paste, and dry it in a warm Oven or Stove.

93. *To make Snow Cream.*

Take a Pint of Cream, and the Whites of three Eggs, one spoonful or two of Rosewater, whip it to a Froth with a Birchen Rod, then cast it off the Rod into a Dish, in the which you have first fastened half a Manchet with some Butter on the bottom, and a long Rosemary sprig in the middle; when you have all cast the Snow on the dish, then garnish it with several sorts of sweet-meats.

94. *To preserve Oranges and Limons that they shall have a Rock Candy on them in the Syrrup.*

Take the fairest and cut them in halves, or if you will do them whole, then cut a little hole in the bottom, so that you may take out all the meat, lay them in water nine days, shifting them twice every day, then boil them in several Waters, till a straw will run through them, then take to every Pound of Orange or Limon one Pound of fine Sugar, and one quart of Water, make your Syrrup, and let your Oranges or Limons boil a while in it, then let them stand five or six days in that Syrrup, then to every Pound, put one Pound more of Sugar into your Syrrup, and boil your Oranges till they be very clear, then take your Oranges out, and boil your Syrrup almost to Candy, and put to them.

95. *To make Sugar Plate.*

Take a little Gum-Dragon laid in steep in Rosewater till it be like Starch, then beat it in a Mortar with some searced Sugar till it come to a perfect Paste, then mould it with Sugar, and make it into what form you please, and colour some of them, lay them in a warm place, and they will dry of themselves.

96. *To make Artificial Walnuts.*

Take some of your Sugar Plate, print it in a Mould fit for a Walnut Kernel, yellow it over with a little Saffron, then take searced Cinamon and Sugar, as much of the one as the other, work it in Paste with some Rosewater, wherein Gum Dragon hath been steeped, and print it in a Mould for a Walnut shell, and when they are dry, close them together over the shell with a little of the Gum water.

97. *To make short Cakes.*

Take a Pint of Ale Yest, and a Pound and half of fresh Butter, melt your Butter, and let it cool a little, then take as much fine Flower as you think will serve, mingle it with the Butter and Yest, and as much Rosewater and Sugar as you think fit, and if you please, some Caraway Comfits, so bake it in little Cakes; they will last good half a year.

98. *To preserve red Roses, which is as good and effectual as any Conserve, and made with less trouble.*

Take Red Rose Buds clipped clean from their Whites one pound, put them into a Skillet with four Quarts of Water, Wine measure, then let them boil very fast till three Quarts be boiled away, then put in three pounds of fine Sugar, and let it boil till it begins to be thick, then put in the Juice of a Limon, and boil it a little longer, and when it is almost cold, put it into Gally-Pots, and strew them over with searced Sugar, and so keep them so long as you please, the longer the better.

99. *A fine Cordial Infusion.*

Take the flesh of a Cock Chick cut in small pieces, and put into a Glass with a wide Mouth, put to it one Ounce of Harts-horn, half an Ounce of Red Coral prepared, with a little large Mace, and a slice or two of Limon, and two Ounces of White Sugar-Candy, stop the Glass close with a Cork, and set it into a Vessel of seething Water, and stuff it round with Hay that it jog not; when you find it to be enough, give the sick Party two spoonfuls at a time.

100. *For a Cough of the Lungs.*

Take two Ounces of Oil of sweet Almonds newly drawn, three spoonfuls of
Colts-foot Water, two spoonfuls of Red Rose-Water, two Ounces of white Sugar-Candy finely beaten; mingle all these together, and beat it one hour with a spoon, till it be very white; then take it often upon a Licoras stick. This is very good.

101. *To preserve Grapes.*

Take your fairest white Grapes and pick them from the stalks, then stone them carefully, and save the Juice, then take a pound of Grapes, a pound of fine Sugar, and a pint of water wherein sliced Pippins have been boiled, strain that water, and with your Sugar and that make a Syrup, when it is well scummed put in your Grapes, and boil them very fast, and when you see they are as clear as glass, and that the Syrup will jelly, put them into Glasses.

102. *To make Collops of Bacon in Sweet-meats.*

Take some Marchpane Paste, and the weight thereof in fine Sugar beaten and searsed, boil them on the fire, and keep them stirring for fear they burn, so do till you find it will come from the bottom of the Posnet, then mould it with fine Sugar like a Paste, and colour some of it with beaten Cinnamon, and put in a little Ginger, then roll it broad and thin, and lay one upon another till you think it be of a fit thickness and cut it in Collops and dry it in an Oven.

103. *To make Violet Cakes.*

Take them clipped clean from the whites and their weight in fine Sugar, wet your Sugar in fair water, and boil it to a Candy height, then put in your Violets, and stir them well together, with a few drops of a Limon, then pour them upon a wet Pye-Plate, or on a slicked paper, and cut them in what form you please; do not let them boil, for that will spoil the colour: Thus you may do with any Herb or Flower, or with any Orange or Limon Pill, and, if you like it, put in a little Musk or Ambergreece.

104. *To preserve white Damsons.*

Take to every pound one pound of fine Sugar and a quarter of a pint of fair water, make your Syrup and scum it well, then take it from the fire, and when it is almost cold put in your Damsons, and let them scald a little, then take them off a while, and then set them on again; when you perceive them to be very clear, put them into Pots or Glasses.

105. *To make a very good Cake.*

Take a peck of Flower, four pound of Currans well washed, dryed and picked, four pounds of Butter, one pound of Sugar, one ounce of Cinnamon, one ounce of Nutmegs, beat the Spice and lay it all night in Rosewater, the next day strain it out, then take one pint and an half of good Ale-Yest the Yolks of 4 Eggs, a pint of Cream, put a pound of the butter into the warmed Cream, put the rest into the Flower in pieces, then wet your Flower with your Cream, and put in your Currans, and a little Salt, and four or five spoonfuls of Caraway-Comfits and your Spice, mix them all and the Yest well together, and let it lie one hour to rise, then make it up and Bake it in a Pan buttered: It may stand two hours.

106. *To make Paste Royal.*

Take Quince Marmalade almost cold, and mould it up with searced Sugar to a Paste, them make it into what form you please and dry them in a Stove.

107. *To make Paste of Pippins coloured with Barberries.*

Take the Pulp of Codled Pippins, and as much of the Juice of Barberries as will colour it, then take the weight of it in fine Sugar, boil it to a Candy height, with a little water, then put in your Pulp beaten very well in a mortar, boil it till it come from the bottom of the Posnet, then dust your Plate with Sugar, and drop them thereon, and dry them in a Stove or warm Oven.

108. *To preserve Barberries.*

Take one Pound of stoned Barberries and twice their weight in fine Sugar, then strip two or three handfuls of Barberries from their stalks, and put them into a Dish with as much Sugar as Barberries, over a Chafing dish of Coals, when you see they are well plumped, strain them, then wet your other Sugar with this, and no Water, boil it and scum it, and then put in your stoned Barberries, and boil them till they are very clear.

109. *To make Jelly of Currans or of any other Fruit.*

Take your Fruit clean picked from the stalks, and put them into a long Gally-pot, and set it into a Kettle of Water close covered; keep the Water boiling till you find the Fruit be well infused, then pour out the clearest, and take the weight of it in fine Sugar, wet your Sugar with Water, and boil it to a Candy height, then put in your clear Liquor, and keep it stirring over a slow fire till you see it will jelly, but do not let it boil; the Pulp which is left of the Liquor, you may make Paste of if you please, as you do the Pippin Paste before named.

110. *To make a Goosberry Fool.*

Take a Pint and an half of Goosberries clean picked from the stalks, put them into a Skillet with a Pint and half of fair Water, scald them till they be very tender, then bruise them well in the Water, and boil them with a Pound and half of fine Sugar till it be of a good thickness, then put to it the Yolks of six Eggs and a Pint of Cream, with a Nutmeg quartered, stir these well together till you think they be enough, over a slow fire, and put it into a Dish, and when it is cold, eat it.

111. *To make perfumed Lozenges.*

Take twelve Grains of Ambergreece, and six grains of Musk, and beat it with some Sugar plate spoken of before, then roule it out in thin Cakes, and make them into what form you please, you may make them round like a Sugar Plumb, and put a Coriander seed in each of them, and so they will be fine Comfits, and you may make them into Lozenges to perfume Wine with.

112. *To Candy Eryngo Roots.*

Take the Roots new gathered, without Knots or Joints, wash them clean, and boil them in several Waters till they are very tender, then wash them well, and dry them in a Cloth, slit them, and take out the Pith, and braid them in Braids as you would a Womans Hair, or else twist them, then take twice their weight in fine Sugar, take half that Sugar, and to every Pound of Sugar, one quarter of a pint of Rosewater and as much fair water, make a syrup of it, and put in your roots and boil them, and when they are very clear, wet the rest of the Sugar with Rosewater, and boil it to a Candy height, then put in the Roots and boil them, and shake them, and when they be enough, take them off, and shake them till they are cold and dry, then lay them upon Dishes or Plates till they are throughly dry, and then put them up; thus you may do Orange or Limon, or Citron Pill, or Potato Roots.

113. *To preserve Goosberries.*

Take your Gooseberries, and stone them, then take a little more than their weight in fine Sugar, then with as much Water as will melt the Sugar, boil it and scum it, then put in your Goosberries, and boil them apace till they be clear, then take up your Goosberries, and put them into Glasses, and boil the Syrup a little more, and put over them.

114. *To make Leach and to colour it.*

Take one Ounce of Isinglass and lay it in Water four and twenty hours, changing the Water three or four times, then take a quart of new Milk, boiled with a little sliced Ginger and a stick of Cinamon, one spoonful of Rosewater, and a quarter of a Pound of Sugar, when it hath boiled a while, put in the Isinglass, and boil it till it be thick, keeping it always stirring, then strain it, and keep it stirring, and when it is cold, you may slice it out, and serve it upon Plates; you may colour it with Saffron, and some with Turnsole, and lay the White and that one upon another, and cut it, and it will look like Bacon; it is good for weak people, and Children that have the Rickets.

115. *To take away the Signs of the Small Pox.*

Take some Spercma-ceti, and twice so much Virgins Wax, melt them together and spread it upon Kids Leather, in the shape of Mask, then lay it upon the Face, and keep it on night and day, it is a very fine Remedy.

116. *For Morphew, or Freckles, and to clear the Skin.*

Take the Blood of any Fowl or Beast, and wipe your Face all over with it every night when you go to bed for a fortnight together, and the next day wash it all off with White Wine, and white Sugar Candy, and sometimes hold your face over the smoke of Brimstone for a while, and shut your eyes, if you add the Juice of a Limon to the white Wine, it will be the better.

117. *To make Almond Butter to look white.*

Take about two Quarts of Water, the bottom of a Manchet, and a Blade of large Mace, boil it half an hour, and let it stand till it be cold, then take a Pound of sweet Almonds blanched, and beaten with Rosewater very fine, so strain them with this Water many times, till you think the virtue is out of them, and that it be a thick Almond Milk, then put it into a Skillet, and make it boiling hot, that it simper, then take a spoonful of the Juice of a Limon, and put into it, stirring of it in, and when you perceive it ready to turn, then take it from the fire, and take a large fine Cloth, and cast your Liquor all over the Cloth with a Ladle, then scrape it altogether into the middle with a Spoon, then tie it hard with a Packthred, so let it hang till the next morning, then put in a Dish, and sweeten it with Rosewater and Sugar, put a little Ambergreece if you please.

118. *For the Ptisick.*

Take a Pottle of small Ale, one Pound of Raisins of the Sun stoned, with a little handful of Peniroyal, boil these together, and add a little Sugar-candy to it, and take five or six spoonfuls at a time four or five times in a day for a good while.

119. *Marmalade of Apricocks.*

Take the ripest and stone them and pare them, and beat them in a Mortar, then boil the Pulp in a Dish over a Chafing-dish of Coals, till it be somewhat dry, then take the weight in fine Sugar, and boil it to a Candy height, with some Rosewater, then put in your Pulp, and boil them together till it will come from the bottom of the Skillet, and always keep it stirring, for fear it burn, then put it into Glasses.

120. *Syrup of Turneps.*

Take of the best and pare them, and bake them in a Pot, then take the clear Juice from them, and with the like weight in fine Sugar make it into a Syrup, and a little Licoras to it, and take it often.

121. *To make a good Jelly.*

Take a lean Pig, dress it clean, and boil it in a sufficient quantity of Fair Water, with four Ounces of green Licoras scraped and bruised, Maidenhair two handfuls, Colts-foot one handful, Currans half a Pound, Dates two Ounces stoned and sliced, Ivory one Ounce, Hartshorn one Ounce, boil these to a strong Jelly, and strain it, and take off the Fat, then put to it half a Pound of Sugar, and half a Pint of white Wine, and so eat it at your pleasure.

122. *A most excellent Cordial proved by very many.*

Take three Grains of East Indian Bezoar, as much of Ambergreece, powder them very fine with a little Sugar, and mingle it with a spoonful and half of the Syrup of the juice of Citrons, one Spoonful of Syrup of Clovegilliflowers, and one spoonful of Cinamon Water, so take it warmed.

123. *To make the black Juice of Licoras.*

Take two Gallons of running Water, three handfuls of unset Hysop, three pounds and half of Licoras scraped, and dried in the Sun and beaten, then cover it close, and boil it almost a whole day in the Water, when it is enough, it will be as thick as Cream, then let it stand all night, the next morning strain it, and put it in several Pans in the Sun to dry, till it work like wax, then mould it with White Sugar Candy beaten and searced, then print it in little Cakes, and print them with Seals, and dry them.

124. *To make Marchpane.*

Take two Pounds of Jordan Almonds, blanch and beat them in a Mortar with Rosewater, then take one Pound and half of Sugar finely searced, when the Almonds are beaten to a fine Paste with the Sugar, then, take it out of the Mortar, and mould it with searced Sugar, and let it stand one hour to cool, then roll it as thin as you would do for a Tart, and cut it round by the Plate, then set an edge about it, and pinch it, then set it on a bottom of Wafers, and bake it a little, then Ice it with Rosewater and Sugar, and the White of an Egg beaten together, and put it into the Oven again, and when you see the Ice rise white and high, take it out, and set up a long piece of Marchpane first baked in the middle of the Marchpane, stick it with several sorts of Comfits, then lay on Leaf-gold with a Feather and the White of an Egg beaten.

125. *To preserve Green Pippins.*

Scald some green Pippins carefully, then peel them, and put them into warm water, and cover them, and let them stand over a slow fire till they are as green as you would have them, and so tender as that a straw may run through them, then to every pound of Apples, take one pound of fine Sugar, and half a pint of water, of which make a Syrup, and when you have scumm'd it clean, put in your Apples, and let them boil a while, then set them by till the next day, then boil them throughly, and put them up.

126. *To preserve Peaches.*

Take your Peaches when you may prick a hole through them, scald them in fair water and rub the Fur off from them with your Thumb, then put them in another warm water over a slow fire, and cover them till they be green, then take their weight in fine Sugar and a little water, boil it and scum it, then put in your Peaches, and boil them till they are clear, so you may do green Plumbs or green Apricocks.

127. *Marmalade of Damsons.*

Take two Pounds of Damsons, and one Pound of Pippins pared and cut in pieces, bake them in an Oven with a little sliced Ginger, when they are tender, poure them into a Cullender, and let the Syrup drop from them, then strain them, and take as much sugar as the Pulp doth weigh, boil it to a Candy height with a little water, then put in your Pulp, and boil it till it will come from the bottom of the Skillet, and so put it up.

128. *Marmalade of Wardens.*

Bake them in an earthen pot, then cut them from the Core and beat them in a Mortar, then take their weight in fine Sugar, and boil it to a Candy height with a little beaten Ginger, and boil it till it comes from the bottom of the Posnet; and so do with Quinces if you please.

129. *Marmalade of green Pippins to look green.*

Scald them as you do to preserve, then stamp them in a Mortar, and take their weight in fine Sugar, boil it to a Candy height with a little water, then boil it and the Pulp together, till it will come from the bottom of Posnet.

130. *To preserve green Walnuts.*

Take them and steep them all night in water, in the morning pare them and boil them in fair water till they be tender, and then stick a Clove into the head of each of them, then take one Pound and half of Sugar to every pound of Walnuts, and to every pound of Sugar one Pint of Rosewater, make a Syrup of it, and scum it, then put in your Walnuts, and boil them very leasurely till they are enough; then put in a little Musk or Ambergreece with a little Rosewater, and boil them a little more, and put them up; it is a very good Cordial, and will keep seven years or more.

131. *To dry old Pippins.*

Pare them, and bore a hole through them with a little Knife or Piercer, and cut some of them in halves, take out the Cores of them as you cut them, then put them into a Syrup of Sugar and water, as much as will cover them in a broad preserving Pan, let them boil so fast as may be; taking them sometimes from the fire, scumming them clean; when you perceive your Apples clear, and Syrup thick, then take them up, and set them into a warm Oven from the Syrup, all night, the next morning turn them, and put them in again, so do till they are dry; if you please to glister some of them, put them into your Candy-pot but one night, and lay them to dry the next day, and they will look like Crystal.

132. *To preserve Bullace as green as grass.*

Take them fresh gathered, and prick them in several places, scald them as you do your green Peaches, then take their weight in fine sugar, and make a Syrup with a little water, then put in your Bullace, and boil them till they be very clear, and the Syrup very thick.

133. *To preserve Medlars.*

Take them at their full growth, pare them as thin as you can, prick them with your Knife, and parboil them reasonable tender, then dry them with a Cloth, and put to them as much clarified sugar as will cover them; let them boil leisurely, turning them often, till they have well taken the sugar, then put them into an earthen Pot, and let them stand till the next day, then warm them again half an hour; then take them up and lay them to drain, then put into that Syrup half a pint of water wherein Pippins have been boiled in slices, and a quarter of a Pound of fresh sugar, boil it, and when it will jelly, put it to the Medlars in Gallipots or Glasses.

134. *To make Conserve of Violets.*

Take a pound clean cut from the whites, stamp them well in a Mortar, and put to them two or three Ounces of white Sugar-Candy, then take it out and lay it upon a sleeked Paper, then take their weight in fine sugar, and boil it to a Candy height with a little water, then put in your Violets, and a little Juice of Limon, and then let them have but one walm or two over the fire, stirring it well; then take it off; and when it is between hot and cold, put it up, and keep it.

135. *To cast all kinds of shapes, what you please, and to colour them.*

Take half a pound of refined Sugar, boil it to a Candy height with as much Rosewater as will melt it, then take moulds made of Alabaster, and lay them in water one hour before you put in the hot Sugar, then when you have put in your Sugar turn the mould about in your hand till it be cool, then take it out of the mould, and colour it according to the nature of the Fruit you would have it resemble.

136. *To dry Pears without Sugar.*

Pare them, and leave the stalks and pipps on them, then bake them in an earthen pot with a little Claret Wine, covered, then drain them from the Syrup, and dry them upon Sieves in a warm Oven, turning them morning and evening, every time you turn them hold them by the stalk and dip them in the Liquor wherein they were baked and flat them every time a little.

If you do them carefully they will look very red and clear and eat moist, when they are dry put them up.

137. *To make Rasberry Wine.*

Take Rasberries and bruise them with the back of a spoon, and strain them, and fill a bottle with the juyce, stop it, but not very close, let it stand four or five days, then pour it from the Grounds into a Bason, and put as much White-wine or Rhenish as your juyce will well colour, then sweeten it with Loaf Sugar, then bottle it and keep it, and when you drink it you may perfume some of it with one of the Lozenges spoken of before.

138. *To preserve Oranges in jelly.*

Take the thickest rind Oranges, chipped very thin, lay them in water three or four days, shifting them twice every day, then boil them in several waters, till you may run a straw through them, then let them lye in a Pan of water all night, then dry them gently in a Cloth, then take to every Pound of Oranges one Pound and an half of Sugar, and a Pint of water, make thereof a syrup; then put in your Oranges, and boil them a little, then set them by till the next day, and boil them again a little, and so do for four or five days together, then boil them till they are very clear, then drain them in a sieve, then take to every Pound of Oranges one quarter of a Pint of water wherein sliced Pippins have been boiled into your syrup, and to every quarter of a Pint of that water, add a quarter of a Pound of fresh Sugar, boil it till it will jelly, then put your Oranges into a Pot or a Glass, and put the jelly over them; you may if you please, take all the Meat out of some of your Oranges at one end, and fill it with preserved Pippin, and if you put in a little Juice of Orange and Limon into your Syrup when it is almost boiled, it will be very fine tasted.

138. [Transcriber's note: so numbered in original] *To make Cristal Jelly.*

Take a Knuckle of Veal and two Calves Feet, lay them in water all night, then boil them in Spring water, till you perceive it to be a thick Jelly, then take them out, and let your Jelly stand till it be cold, then take the clearest, and put it into a Skillet, and sweeten it with Rosewater and fine Sugar, and a little whole Spice, and boil them together a little, and so eat it when it is cold.

139. *To make* China-*Broth.*

Take three Ounces of *China* sliced thin, and three Pints of fair water, half an ounce of Harts-horn, let it steep together twelve hours, then put in a Red

Cock cut in pieces and bruised, one Ounce of Raisins of the Sun stoned, one ounce of Currans, one ounce of Dates stoned, one Parsley root, one Fennel-root, the Pith being taken out, a little Burrage and Bugloss, and a little Pimpernel, two Ounces of Pearl Barley; boil all these together till you think they be well boiled, then strain it out.

140. *To make Court Perfumes.*

Take three Ounces of Benjamin, lay it all night in Damask Rose buds clean cut from the white, beat them very fine in a stone Mortar till it come to a Paste, then take it out and mix it with a dram of Musk finely beaten, as much Civet, mould them up with a little searced Sugar, and dry them between Rose Leaves each of them, then dry them very well and keep them to burn, one at a time is sufficient.

141. *A Syrup for a Cold.*

Take Long-wort of the Oak, Sage of *Jerusalem*, Hysop, Colts-foot, Maidenhair, Scabious, Horehound, one handful of each, four Ounces of Licoras scraped, two Ounces of Anniseeds bruised, half a pound of Raisins of the Sun stoned, put these together into a Pipkin with two quarts of Spring water, let them stand all night to infuse close stopped, when it is half boiled away, strain it out, and put to it to every pint of liquor a pound of Sugar and boil it to a Syrup.

142. *To make white Marmalade of Quinces.*

Coddle them so tender that a straw may run thorow them, then take grated Quinces and strain the Juice from them, then slice your scalded Quinces thin and weigh them, and take a little above their weight in fine

Sugar, wet your Sugar with the raw juice, boil it and scum it, then put in your sliced Quinces and boil them up quick till they jelly, then put them into Glasses.

143. *The white juice of Licoras.*

Take one pound of Licoras clean scraped, cut it thin and short, and dry it in an Oven, then beat it fine in a Mortar, then put it into a stone Jugg, and put thereto of the water of Colts-foot, Scabius, Hysop and Horehound, as much as will stand four fingers deep above the Licoras, then set this Jugg, close stopped, into a Kettle of water, and keep the water boiling, let it be stuffed round with hay that it jog not, let it stand so four hours, and so do every other day for the space of ten days; then strain it into a dish, set the dish over boiling water, and let it vapour away till it be thick, then add to it one pound of fine Sugar-Candy, the best and whitest you can get, beaten very well, then put it into several dishes and dry it in the Sun, or in a warm Oven, beating it often with bone knives till it be stiff, then take as much Gum Dragon steeped in Rose-water as will make it pliable to your hand, then make it into little Rolls, and add two grains of Musk or Ambergreece and a few drops of Oyl of Anniseed, and so make them into little Cakes, and print them with a Seal and then dry them.

144. *To dry Plumbs naturally.*

Take of any sort and prick them and put them into the bottom of a Sieve dusted with Flower to keep them from sticking, let them stand in a warm Oven all night, the next morning turn them upon a clean Sieve, and so do every day till you see that they are very dry.

145. *To dry preserved Pears.*

Wash them from their Syrup, then take some fine Sugar and boil it to a Candy height with a little water, then put in your Pears, and shake them very well up and down, then lay them upon the bottom of a Sieve, and dry them in a warm Oven and so keep them.

146. *To make little Cakes with Almonds.*

Put into a little Rosewater two grains of Ambergreece, then take a pound of blanched Almonds and beat them with this Rosewater, then take a Pound of your finest Sugar, beaten and searced, and when your Almonds are well beaten, mix some of the Sugar with them, then make your Cakes, and lay them on Wafer sheets; and when they are half baked, take the rest of the Sugar, being boiled to a Candy height with a little Rosewater, and so with a Feather wash them over with this, and let them stand a while longer.

147. *To make very pretty Cakes that will keep a good while.*

Take a Quart of fine Flower and the yolks of 4 Eggs, a quarter of a pound of Sugar, and a little Rosewater, with some beaten Spice, and as much Cream as will work it into a Paste, work it very well and beat it, then rowl it as thin as possible, and cut them round with a Spur, such as the Pastry Cooks do use; then fill them with Currans first plumped a little in Rosewater and Sugar, so put another sheet of Paste over them and close them, prick them, and bake them but let not your Oven be too hot; you may colour some of them with Saffron if you please, and some of them you may ice over with Rosewater and Sugar, and the White of an Egg beaten together.

148. *To make a Paste to wash your hands withal.*

Take a Pound of bitter Almonds, blanch them and beat them very fine in a Mortar with four Ounces of Figgs, when it is come to a paste, put it into a Gallipot and keep it for your use; a little at a time will serve.

149. *To keep Flowers all the Year.*

Take any sort of pretty Flowers you can get, and have in readiness some Rosewater made very slippery by laying Gum Arabick therein.

Dip your Flowers very well, and swing it out again, and stick them in a sieve to dry in the Sun, some other of them you may dust over with fine Flower, and some with searced Sugar, after you have wetted them, and so dry them.

Either of them will be very fine, but those with Sugar will not keep so well as the other; they are good to set forth Banquets, and to garnish Dishes, and will look very fresh, and have their right smell.

150. *Conserve of Barberries.*

Take Barberries, infuse them in a pot as other Fruits spoken of before, then strain them, and to every pound of liquor take two pounds of Sugar, boil them together over the fire till it will come from the bottom of the Posnet, and then put it into Gally-pots and keep it with fine Sugar strewed over it.

151. *To preserve Barberries without Fire.*

Take your fairest bunches and lay a Lay of fine Sugar into the bottom of the pot, and then a Lay of Barberries, and then Sugar again, till all be in, and be sure to cover them deep with Sugar last of all, and cover your pot with a bladder wet and tyed on, that no Air get in, and they will keep and be good, and much better to garnish dishes with than pickled Barberries, and are very pleasant to eat.

152. *To Candy Almonds to look as though they had their Shells on.*

Take Jordan Almonds and blanch them, then take fine Sugar, wet it with water, and boil it to a Candy height, colour it with Cochineal, and put in a grain of Ambergreece; when you see it at a Candy height, put in your Almonds well dried from the Water, and shake them over the fire till you see they are enough, then lay them in a Stove or some other warm place.

153. *To Candy Carrot Roots.*

Take of the best and Boil them tender then pare them, and cut them in such pieces as you like; then take fine Sugar boiled to a Candy height with a little Water, then put in your Roots, and boil them till you see they will Candy; but you must first boil them with their weight in Sugar and some Water, or else they will not be sweet enough; when they are enough, lay them into a Box, and keep them dry: thus you may do green Peascods when they are very young, if you put them into boiling water, and let them boil close covered till they are green, and then boiled in a Syrup, and then the Candy, they will look very finely, and are good to set forth Banquets, but have no pleasant taste.

154. *To make Syrup of Violets.*

Take Violets clipped clean from the Whites, to every Ounce of Violets take two Ounces of Water, so steep them upon Embers till the Water be as blew as a Violet, and the Violets turned white, then put in more Violets into the same Water, and again the third time, then take to every Quart of Water four Pounds of fine Sugar, and boil it to a Syrup, and keep it for your use; thus you may also make Syrup of Roses.

155. *To make a Syrup for any Cough.*

Take four Ounces of Licoras scraped and bruised, Maidenhair one Ounce, Aniseeds half an Ounce, steep them in Spring water half a day, then boil it half away; the first quantity of water which you steep them in must be four Pints, and when it is half boiled away, then add to it one Pound of fine Sugar, and boil it to a Syrup, and take two spoonfuls at a time every night when you go to rest.

156. *A pretty Sweet-meat with Roses and Almonds.*

Take half a Pound of Blanched Almonds beaten very fine with a little Rosewater, two Ounces of the Leaves of Damask Roses beaten fine, then take half a pound of Sugar, and a little more, wet it with water, and boil it to a Candy height, then put in your Almonds and Roses, and a grain of Musk or Ambergreece, and let them boil a little while together, and then put it into Glasses, and it will be a fine sort of Marmalade.

157. *The best sort of Hartshorn Jelly to serve in a Banquet.*

Take six Ounces of Hartshorn, put it into two Quarts of Water and let it infuse upon Embers all night, then boil it up quick, and when you find by the Spoon you stir it with, that it will stick to your mouth, if you do touch it, and that you find the Water to be much wasted, strain it out, and put in a little more than half a Pound of fine Sugar, a little Rosewater, a Blade of Mace, and a Stick of Cinamon, the Juice of as many Limons will give it a good taste, with two Grains of Ambergreece, set it over a slow fire, and do not let it boil, but when you find it to be very thick in your mouth, then put it softly into Glasses; and set it into a Stove, and that will make it to jelly the better.

158. *To make Orange or Limon Chips.*

Take the parings of either of these cut thin, and boil them in several waters till they be tender, then let them lie in cold water a while, then take their weight in Sugar or more, and with as much water as will wet it, boil it and scum it, then drain your Chips from the cold water, and put them into a Gally-pot; and pour this Syrup boiling hot upon them, so let them stand till the next day, then heat the Syrup again and pour over them, so do till you see they are very clear, every day do so till the Syrup be very thick, and then lay them out in a Stove to dry.

159. *To make Cakes of Almonds in thin slices.*

Take four Ounces of Jordan Almonds, blanch them in cold water, and slice them thin the long way, then mix them with little thin pieces of Candied Orange and Citron Pill, then take some fine Sugar boiled to a Candy height with some water, put in your Almonds, and let them boil till you perceive they will Candy, then with a spoon take them out, and lay them in little Lumps upon a Pie-plate or sleeked Paper, and before they be quite cold strew Caraway Comfits on them, and so keep them very dry.

160. *To make Chips of any Fruit.*

Take any preserved Fruit, drain it from the syrup, and cut it thin, then boil Sugar to a Candy height, and then put your Chips therein, and shake them up and down till you see they will Candy, and then lay them out; or take raw Chips of Fruit boiled first in Syrup, and then a Candy boiled, and put over them hot, and so every day, till they begin to sparkle as they lie, then take them out, and dry them.

161. *To preserve sweet Limons.*

Take the fairest, and chip them thin, and put them into cold water as you chip them, then boil them in several waters till a straw may run through them, then to every pound of limon, take a pound and half of fine Sugar, and a pint of water, boil it together, and scum it, then let your Limons scald in it a little, and set them by till the next day, and every other day heat the syrup only and put to them; so do 9 times, and then at last boil them in the Syrup till they be clear, then take them out, and put them into Pots, and boil the Syrup a little more, and put to them; if you will have them in Jelly, make your Syrup with Pippin water.

162. *To make a Custard for a Consumption.*

Take four Quarts of Red Cows Milk, four Ounces of Conserve of Red Roses, prepared Pearl, prepared Coral, and white Amber, of each one Dram, two Ounces of white Sugar Candy, one grain of Ambergreece, put these into an earthen pot with some leaf gold, and the yolks and whites of twelve Eggs, a little Mace and Cinamon, and as much fine Sugar as will sweeten it well; Paste the Pot over and bake it with brown Bread, and eat of it every day so long as it will last.

163. *To make Chaculato.*

Take half a Pint of Claret Wine, boil it a little, then scrape some Chaculato very fine and put into it, and the Yolks of two Eggs, stir them well together over a slow Fire till it be thick, and sweeten it with Sugar according to your taste.

164. *To dry any Sort of Plumbs.*

Take to every pound of Plumbs three quarters of a pound of Sugar, boil it to a Candy height with a little water, then put in your Plumbs ready stoned, and let them boil very gently over a slow fire, if they be white ones they may boil a little faster, then let them by till the next day, then boil them well, and take them often from the fire for fear of breaking, let them lie in their Syrup for four or five days, then lay them out upon Sieves to dry, in a warm Oven or Stove, turning them upon clean Sieves twice every day, and fill up all the broken places, and put the skins over them, when they are dry, wash off the clamminess of them with warm water, and dry them in the Oven, and they will look as though the dew were upon them.

165. *To make Jelly of Quinces.*

Take your Quinces, pare them and core them, and cut them in quarters, then put them into a new earthen pot with a narrow mouth, put in some of the cores in the bottom, and then the Quinces, paste it up and bake it with brown Bread, then run it thorough a bagg of boulting stuff as fast as you can, and crush it pretty hard, so long as it will run clear, to every pound of it take a pound of fine Sugar, and put into it, and let it stand till it be dissolved, then set it over a slow fire, and scum it well, and keep it stirring till it jelly, then put it into Glasses and keep it in a stove.

166. *To make a Posset.*

Take a Quart of White-wine and a quart of Water, boil whole Spice in them, then take twelve Eggs and put away half the Whites, beat them very well, and take the Wine from the fire, then put in your Eggs and stir them very well, then set it on a slow fire, and stir it till it be thick, sweeten it with Sugar, and strew beaten Spice thereon, then serve it in.

You may put in Ambergreece if you like it, or one perfumed Lozenge.

167. *To make a Sack Posset.*

Take two quarts of Cream and boil it with Whole Spice, then take twelve Eggs well beaten and drained, take the Cream from the fire, and stir in the Eggs, and as much Sugar as will sweeten it, then put in so much Sack as will make it taste well, and set it on the fire again, and let it stand a while, then take a Ladle and raise it up gently from the bottom of the Skillet you make it in, and break it as little as you can, and so do till you see it be thick enough; then put it into a Bason with the Ladle gently; if you do it too much it will whey, and that is not good.

168. *Another way for a Posset.*

Boil a Quart of Cream as for the other, then take the Yolks of fourteen Eggs and four Whites, beat them and strain them, take the Cream from the fire, and stir in your Eggs, then have your Sack warmed in a Bason, and when the Cream and Eggs are well mixed, put it to the Sack, and sweeten it to your taste with fine Sugar, and let it stand over a Skillet of seething water for a while.

169. *To preserve Pippins in thin slices in Jelly.*

Take of the fairest Pippins, pare them, and slice them into cold water, to every pound of Pippins take a pound of Sugar, and a Pint of Water, boil it and scum it, then shake your Pippins clean from the water, and put them into the Syrup, boil them very clear and apace, then put in some thin Chips, or Orange or Citron preserved, and to one Pound of Pippin, put the Juice of two Oranges and one Limon, then boil them a little longer till you see they will jelly, and then put them into Glasses, but take heed you lay them in carefully, and lay the Chips here and there between, and warm the Jelly and put softly over them.

170. *To preserve Currans in Jelly.*

Take the fairest and pick them from the Stalks, and stone them, and take their weight in sugar, wet it with water, boil it and scum it, then put in your Currans, and boil them up quick, shake them often and scum them, and when they will jelly, they are enough; then put them into Glasses; thus you may do white and red both, and they will be in a stiff Jelly, and cut very well, do not cover them before they be cold.

171. *To preserve ripe Apricocks.*

Take them and stone them, and weigh them, and to every Pound of Apricocks take a Pound of fine Sugar beaten small, then pare your Fruit, and as you pare them, cast some Sugar over them, and so do till all be done, then set them on the fire, and let the Sugar melt but gently, then boil them a little in the Syrup, and set them by till the next day, then boil them quick, and till they be very clear, then put them in Pots, and boil the Syrup a little more, and put it to them, if you would have them in Jelly, you must put some of the Infusion of Goosberries, or of Pippins into your Syrup, and add more Sugar to it.

172. *To preserve Cornelions.*

Take the fairest and weigh them, then take their weight in Sugar, and lay a Lay of Sugar into the Pan, and then lay a Lay of Cornelions till all be in, and let your last Lay be Sugar, then put a little water into the midst of the Pan, and set it on the fire, and when the Sugar is melted boil them up quick, and take them often and shake them, and scum them, when you do perceive them to be very clear, they are enough.

173. *To make Marmalade of Cornelions.*

Take them and stone them, and weigh them, and to every pound of Fruit take a pound of Sugar, wet it with water, and boil it to a Candy height, then put in your Fruit and boil it very clear and quick, and shake it often, and scum it clean; when you see it very clear and very thick, it is enough; you must keep it in a Stove or some warm place.

174. *To preserve Damsons.*

Take the fairest, not too ripe, and take their weight in Sugar, wet your Sugar with a little water, boil it and scum it, then put in your Damsons and boil them a little, then set them by till the next day, then boil them till they be very clear, and take them from the fire sometimes, and let them stand a while to keep them from breaking, when they are clear, take them out, and put them into Glasses, and boil the Syrup to a Jelly and pour on them; be very careful how you take them to put them into your Pots or Glasses for fear of breaking them.

175. *To make Orange Marmalade.*

Take half a Pound of Orange Chips tenderly boiled in several waters, and beaten fine in a Mortar, then take a Pound of fine sugar, wet it with water, boil it and scum it, then put in your Orange, and half a Pound of Pippin also beaten fine, and let them boil together till they are very clear; then put in the Juice of one Orange and one Limon, and stir it well, and let it boil a while longer, and then take it off and put it into Glasses.

176. *To make Jelly of Pippins.*

Take Pippins, pare them thin into a long Gallipot, and set that into boiling water close covered, and so let it stand three or four hours, they must be sliced thin as well as pared; when you think they are infused enough, pour the Liquor from them, and to every Pint, take a pound of Sugar double refined and put it into your Liquor, boil them together till you find it will Jelly, then put little small pieces of Orange Pill into it finely shred, the Juice of one Orange and one Limon, and let it boil a little longer, and so put it into Glasses, and set them into a Stove, with the Pulp that is left you may make Paste if you please.

177. *To candy Angelica.*

Take the tender green stalks and boil them in water till they be tender, then peel them, and put them into another warm water, and cover them till they are very green over a slow fire, then lay them on a clean Cloth to dry, then take their weight in fine Sugar, and boil it to a Candy height with some Rosewater, then put in your stalks, and boil them up quick, and shake them often and when you judge they be enough, lay them on a Pie-plate, and open them with a little stick, and so they will be hollow, and some of them you may braid, and twist some of them, so keep them dry.

178. *To make Seed-stuff of Rasberries.*

Take Rasberries and bruise them, and take their weight in fine Sugar, and boil it to a Candy height with a little water, then put in your bruised Rasberries, and boil them till you see they will jelly very well.

179. *To make Syrup of Gilly-flowers.*

Take Clove-gilly-flowers, and cut them from the Whites, then take their weight in Sugar beaten fine, then put a little sugar into your Gally-pot, and then a Lay of Flowers, and then sugar again, till all be spent, and let sugar be the last, then put in a Clove or two, according to your quantity, and a little Malago Sack; and so tie your Pot up close, and set it into a Pot or Kettle of boiling water, and let them stand till they are infused; then poure out the Liquor and strain the rest, but not too hard, then take this liquor and vapour it away over seething water till it be of a good thickness, then take your strained Gilliflowers and put them into a Pot with some White-wine Vinegar, and cover them over with fine Sugar, and so keep them; they are a better Sallad than those you pickle up alone; as you make this, you may make syrup of any Herbs or Flowers.

180. *To make most excellent Cake.*

Take a strik'd Peck of Flower, six pounds of Currans, half an Ounce of Mace, half an Ounce of Cinamon, a quarter of an Ounce of Cloves, as much of Nutmeg, half a pound of fine Sugar, and as much Rosewater as you please; beat your Spice, and put that and your Fruits with a little Salt into your Flower, then take Cream or new Milk as much as you think fit, dissolve thereinto two pounds of fresh Butter, then put it in a Basin with the sugar and a Pint of Sack, knead it with a Wine-Pint of Ale-Yest, knead it till it rise under your hand, let all things be ready and your Oven hot before you go to knead the Cake.

181. *To make Pomatum the best way.*

Take the Caul of a Lamb new killed, pick it clean from the Skin, and lay it in Spring-water nine days, shifting it every day twice, then melt it, then take yellow Snails, stamp them, and put them into a Glass with Rosewater four days, stop the Glass and shake it three or four times a day, then take white Lilly roots, stamp them, and strain them, put the Juice of them into the Glass with the Snails, then set a Skillet on the fire with fair water, and let it boil, then put your dried Lambs Caul into an earthen basin, and let it melt, then take your Glass with Snails and roots, and drain it through a thick cloth, then put it into that tried stuff, then take half an Ounce of white Sugar-Candy unbeaten put it in, and stir it over the fire, till that be dissolved, then take it from the fire, and put in three Ounces of sweet Almonds, keep it boiling and stirring a little longer, then take it off, and let it stand till it be reasonably cool, then beat it with a wooden Slice till it be very white, then put in a little Rosewater, and beat it a little longer, and then keep it in Gallipots; you must put in a crust of bread when you melt it in the Skillet, and when the Sugar-Candy goes in, take it out.

182. *To make the Bean Bread.*

Take a pound of the best Jordan Almonds; blanch them in cold water, and slice them very thin the long way of the Almond with a wet Knife, then take a pound of double refined Sugar well beaten, and mix with your Almonds, then take the White of one Egg beaten with two spoonfuls of Rosewater, and as the Froth ariseth, cast it all over your Almonds with a Spoon, then mix them well together, and lay them upon Wafer sheets, upon flowered

Plates, and shape them as you please with your knife and your fingers; then strew Caraway Comfits, and Orange and Citron Pill cut thin, or some Coriander Comfits, so set them into an Oven not too hot, and when they have stood about half an hour, raise them from their Plates, and mend what you find amiss before they be too dry, then set them into the Oven again, and when they are quite dry, break away the Wafers with your fingers, and then clip them neatly with a pair of Scizzers, and lay on some Leaf-Gold if you please.

183. *To make an excellent Cake with Caraway Comfits.*

Take five Pounds of Manchet Paste mingled very stiff and light without Salt, cover it, and let it be rising half an hour, when your Oven is almost hot, take two pounds and half of Butter, very good, and melt it, and take five Eggs, Yolks and Whites beaten, and half a pound of Sugar, mingle them all together with your Paste, and let it be as lithe as possible you can work it, and when your Oven is hot and swept, strew into your Cake one Pound of Caraway Comfits, then butter a baking-Pan, and bake it in that, let it stand one hour and quarter; when you draw it, lay a course Linnen Cloth and a Woollen one over it, so let it lie till it be cold, then put it into an Oven the next day, for a little time, and it will eat as though it were made of Almonds, you must put in your Sugar after your Butter.

184. *To make Diet Bread or Jumbolds.*

Take a Quart of fine Flower, half a Pound of fine Sugar, Caraway seeds, Coriander seeds and Aniseeds bruised, of each one Ounce, mingle all these together, then take the Yolks of eight Eggs, and the Whites of three, beat them well with four spoonfuls of Rosewater, and so knead these all together and no other Liquor, when it is well wrought, lay it for one hour in a linnen cloth before the Fire, then rowl it out thin, tie them in Knots and prick them with a Needle, lay them upon Butter'd Plates, and bake them in an Oven not too hot.

185. *To make Cider or Perry as clear as Rock water.*

Take two Quarts of Cider, half a Pint of Milk, put them both in an Hipocras bag, and when it runs clear, bottle it up, and when it is a Month old, it will sparkle in the Glass as you drink it.

186. *To make Almond Bread.*

Take a pound of Almonds blanched, and beaten with Rosewater, then take a pound of Sugar beaten fine, and a little grated Bread finely searced, put them into a Platter with your Almonds, and stir them well together, set them over a Chafing dish of Coals, and boil them till they are as stiff as Paste, stirring them continually, then mould them well and put them in what shape you you please; print them, and set them into some warm place to dry.

187. *To make good Almond Milk.*

Take Jordan Almonds blanched and beaten with Rose water, then strain them often with fair water, wherein hath been boiled Violet Leaves and Sliced Dates; when your Almonds are strained, take the Dates and put to it some Mace, Sugar, and a little Salt, warm it a little, and so drink it.

188. *To make white Leach.*

Take sweet Almonds blanched and beaten with Rosewater, then strained with fair water, wherein hath been boiled Aniseeds and Ginger, put to it as much cream, wherein pure Isinglass hath been boiled, as will make it stiff, and as much Sugar as you please; let it be scalding hot, then run it through a strainer, and when it is cold, slice it out, it is very good for a weak body.

189. *To make Red Leach or Yellow.*

Red by putting Tornsel into it, or Cochineal; Yellow by putting Saffron in it.

190. *Cinamon or Ginger Leach.*

Take your Spices beaten and searced, and mix them with your searced Sugar, mould them up with Gum Arabick infused in Rosewater, and so print them and dry them.

191. *To make Leach of Dates.*

Take your Dates stoned and peeled very clean within, beat them fine with Sugar, Ginger and Cinamon, and a little Rosewater till it will work like Paste, then print them and keep them dry.

192. *To make fine Cakes.*

Take a Quart of Flower, a Pound of sugar, a Pound of Butter, with three or four Yolks of Eggs, a little Rosewater, and a spoonful of Yest, then roul them out thin, while the Paste is hot, prick them, and set them into the Oven not too hot.

193. *To make Cornish Cakes.*

Take Claret Wine, the Yolks of Eggs, and Mace beaten fine, and some Sugar and Salt, mingle all these with Flower and a little Yeast, knead it as stiff as you can, then put in Butter, and knead it stiff again, and then shape them and bake them.

194. *A Cordial Syrup.*

Take one Pound of Juice of Burrage, and half so much of the Juice of Balm, boil them together, and when the grossness of the Juice ariseth, then put in the Whites of two Eggs beaten with Rosewater, and when you see them begin to grow hard, put in a little Vinegar, let them boil together, and scum it clean, and run it through a Jelly-Bag, then set it over the fire again, and add to it one Pound of fine Sugar, and a little Saffron, and so boil it till you think it be enough.

195. *For a Consumption.*

Take of Harts-tongue and Maidenhair, of each one handful, Hysop and Balm, of each half a handful, Licoras sliced, one Ounce, Piony Root one Ounce, boil these together in two Pints and half of Spring water until it be half consumed, then strain the Liquor from the Herbs, then take four Ounces of Currans washed clean, dried and beaten in a Mortar, boil them in the Liquor a little while, then strain it, and put to the Liquor half a Pound of Sugar, and so boil it to a Syrup, and take often of it.

196. *For a Consumption.*

Take a Pint of good Wine-Vinegar, and half a Pint of Colts-foot-water, half a Pound of Figs well bruised, then strain it, and boil it with a Pound of Sugar to a thick Syrup.

197. *A very good Perfume.*

Six Spoonfuls of Rosewater, Musk, Ambergreece and Civet, of each two Grains, a little Sugar beaten fine, mould them up together with Gum-Dragon steeped in Rosewater, make them in little Cakes and dry them.

198. *A Cordial to cause sleep.*

Two spoonfuls of Poppy water, two spoonfuls of Red Rosewater, one spoonful of Clove-Gillyflower Syrup, and a little Diascordium, mingle them together, and take them at the time of rest.

199. *To perfume Gloves.*

Take four Grains of Musk and grind it with Rosewater, and also eight Grains of Civet, then take two spoonfuls of Gum dragon steeped all night in Rosewater, beat these to a thin Jelly, putting in half a spoonful of Oil of Cloves, Cinamon and Jessamine mixed together, then take a Spunge and dip it therin, and rub the Gloves all over thin, lay them in a dry clean place eight and forty hours; then rub them with your hands till they become limber.

200. *A very good Perfume to burn.*

Take 2 ounces of the Powder of Juniper Wood, 1 Ounce of Benjamin, one Ounce of Storax, 6 drops of oil of Limons, as much oil of Cloves, 10 grains of Musk, 6 of Civet, mold them up with a little Gum dragon steeped in Rosewater, make them in little Cakes, and dry them between Rose Leaves, your Juniper wood must be well dried, beaten and searced.

201. *To preserve Cherries in Jelly.*

Take fair ripe Cherries, and stone them, then take a little more than their weight in fine Sugar, then take the juyce of some other Cherries, and put a spoonful of it in the bottom of the Posnet, then put some of your Sugar beaten fine into the Posnet with it, and then a little more juyce, then put in your Cherries, then put in Sugar, and then juyce, and then Cherries again, thus do till you have put in all, then let them boil apace till the Sugar be melted, shaking them sometimes, then take them from the fire, and let them stand close covered one hour, then boil them up quick till the Syrup will jelly.

202. *To dry Apricocks or Pippins to look as clear as Amber.*

Take Apricocks and take out the Stones, and take Pippins and cut them in halves and core them, let your Apricocks be pared also; lay these Fruits in an earthen dish, and strew them over with fine Sugar, set them into a warm Oven, and as the Liquor comes from them put it away, when all the Liquor is come away turn them and strew them thick with Sugar on every side, set them into the Oven again, and when the Sugar is melted lay them on a dry dish, and set them in again, and every day, turn them till they be quite dry, Thus you may dry any sort of Plumbs or Pears as well as the other, and they will look very clear.

203. *To dry Pears or Pippins without Sugar.*

Take of the fairest and lay them in sweetwort two or three days, then lay them in a broad preserving Pan of earth, and bake them, but let the Oven be but gently hot, then lay them upon lattice Sieves and set them into a warm Oven, and turn them twice a day till they are dry.

204. *The Spanish Candy.*

Take any sort of Flowers well picked and beaten in a Mortar, and put them into a Syrup, so much as the Flowers will stain, boil them, and stir them till you see it will turn Sugar again, then pour it upon a wet trencher, and when it is cold cut it into Lozenges, and that which remaineth in the bottom of the Posnet scrape it clean out, and beat it and searce it, then work it with some Gum Dragon steeped in Rosewater and a little Ambergreece, so make it into what shape you please, and dry it.

205. *To make Naples Bisket.*

Take four Ounces of Pine Apple seeds, two Ounces of sweet Almonds blanched, the Whites of two Eggs, one spoonful of Ale-Yeast, one spoonful of Rice Flower, one spoonful of sweet Cream, beat all these together in a Mortar, then add to it Musk or Ambergreece, drop it upon a Pie-plate, and make it in what shape you please, and so bake it.

206. *To make Italian Bisket.*

Take Sugar searced fine, and beat in a Mortar with Gum Dragon steeped in

216. *To dry Apricocks.*

Take your fairest Apricocks and stone them, then weigh them, and as you pare them, throw them into cold water, have in readiness their weight in fine sugar, wet it with some of the water they lie in, and boil it to a Candy height, then put in your Apricocks, and boil them till they are clear, when they have lain three or four days in the Syrup, lay them out upon Glasses to dry in a stove, and turn them twice a day.

217. *To make rough Marmalade of Cherries.*

Stone your Cherries, and infuse them in a long Gallipot in a Kettle of boiling water, when they are all to pieces, then take their weight in fine Sugar boiled to a Candy height with a little water, then put in your Apricocks and stir them over a slow fire, but do not let it boil, when it will jelly, put it into Glasses.

218. *To make smooth Marmalade of Cherries.*

Infuse them as you do the other, then strain them hard, and boil the Juice with a Candy as you do the other.

219. *To make white Trencher-Plates which may be eaten.*

Take two Eggs beaten very well, Yolks and Whites, two spoonfuls of Sack, one spoonful of Rosewater, and so much flower as will make it into a stiff Paste, then roule it thin, and then lay it upon the outsides of Plates well-buttered, cut them fit to the Plates, and bake them upon them, then take them forth, and when they are cold, take a pound of double refin'd

Sugar beaten and searced, with a little Ambergreece, the White of an Egg and Rosewater, beat these well together, and Ice your Plates all over with it, and set them into the Oven again till they be dry.

220. *To make the Froth Posset.*

Take three Pints of Cream or new Milk, set it on the fire, then take sixteen Eggs and put the Whites into a Basin very deep, and beat the Yolks by themselves, make a Custard with them, and the Cream which is on the fire, then beat the Yolks to a Froth with a little Sack, and a little Sugar, when it is a thick Froth, cast it into another Dish with a Spoon, then take half a Pint of Sack, and sweeten it with Sugar, set it on a Chafing-dish of Coals in a large Basin, when it is hot, put in as much Froth as the Sack will receive, stir it in very well, then take your Custard and pour upon it, stir it all one way when you put it in, then if the Froth do not cover the top of the Posset, put in more, and stir it very well, and cover it close with a warm Dish, let it stand a while upon Coals, but not too hot; you may know when it is enough by putting your Spoon into the Basin, for then it will be clear in the bottom, Curd in the middle, and Froth on the top.

221. *To make* Banbury *Cakes.*

Make a Posset of Sack and Cream, then take a Peck of fine Flower, half an Ounce of Mace, as much of Nutmeg, as much of Cinamon, beat them and searce them, two pounds of Butter, ten Eggs, leaving out half their Whites, one Pint and half of Ale-Yest, beat your Eggs very well, and strain them, then put your Yest, and some of the Posset to the Flower, stir them together, and put in your Butter cold in little pieces, but your Posset must be scalding hot; make it into a Paste, and let it lie one hour in a warm Cloth to rise, then put in ten pounds of Currans washed and dried very well, a little

Musk and Ambergreece dissolved in Rosewater, put in a little Sugar among your Currans break your Paste into little pieces, when you go to put in your Currans, then lay a Lay of broken Paste, and then a Lay of Currans till all be in, then mingle your Paste and Currans well together, and keep out a little of your Paste in a warm Cloth to cover the top and bottom of your Cake, you must rowl the Cover very thin, and also the Bottom, and close them together over the Cake with a little Rosewater; prick the top and bottom with a small Pin or Needle, and when it is ready to go into the Oven, cut in the sides round about, let it stand two hours, then Ice it over with Rosewater or Orange Flower and Sugar, and the White of an Egg, and harden it in the Oven.

222. *To make* Cambridge *Almond Butter.*

Take a Quart of Cream and sixteen Eggs well beaten, mix them together and strain them into a Posnet, set them on a soft fire, and stir them continually; when it is ready to boil, put in half a quarter of a Pint of Sack, and stir it till it run to a Curd, then strain the Whey from it as much as may be, then beat four Ounces of blanched Almonds with Rosewater, then put the Curd and beaten Almonds and half a pound of fine Sugar into a Mortar, and beat them well together, then put it into Glasses and eat it with bread, it will keep a Fortnight.

223. *To make a Sack Posset without Milk or Bread.*

Take a Quart of Ale and half a Pint of Sack, boil them with what spice you please, then take three quarters of a pound of sugar, and twenty Eggs, Yolks and Whites well beaten and strained, then take four Ounces of Almonds blanched and beaten with Rosewater, put them to the Eggs, and put them to the other things in the Posnet upon the fire, and keep them stirring, and when it boileth up, put it into a Bason, and strew on beaten spice and sugar, you must also sweeten it when the Eggs go in.

224. *To preserve Figs and dry them.*

To every pound of your large ripe English Figs, take a pound of Sugar, and one Pint of Water boil your Sugar and Water, and scum it, then put in your Figs, and boil them very well till they are tender & clear; boil them very fast, when they have been in the Syrup a week, boil some sugar to a Candy height, and put in the Figs, and when you perceive they are enough, lay them out to dry.

225. *To pickle Mushromes.*

Take them of one nights growth, and peel them inside and outside, boil them in Water and Salt one hour, then lay them out to cool, then make a pickle of White Wine and White Wine Vinegar, and boil in it whole Cloves, Nutmegs, Mace, and Ginger sliced, and some whole Pepper, when it is cold, put them into it, and keep them for Sauces of several Meats; and if you would dress them to eat presently, put them in a Dish over a Chafingdish of Coals without any Liquor, and the fire will draw out their natural Liquor, which you must pour away, then put in whole Spice, Onions and Butter, with a little Wine, and so let them stew a while, then serve it in.

226. *To preserve whole Quinces to look red.*

When they are pared and cored, put them into cold water, and for every Pound of Quince take one Pound of Sugar, and a Pint of Water, make a Syrup thereof, then put in your Quinces, and set them on a slow fire, close covered, till you see they are of a good Colour and very tender, then take them out, and boil your Syrup till it will Jelly.

227. *To make very good Marmalade of Quinces to look red.*

Weigh your Quinces and pare them, cut them in quarters and core them, and keep them in cold water, then take their weight in sugar, and a little water, and boil it, and scum it, then put in your Quinces, and set them on a slow fire, close covered, till you see it of a good colour, then uncover it, and boil it up very quick till you find that it will jelly very well.

228. *To make Musk Sugar.*

Bruise six grains of Musk and tie them in a piece of Tiffany, lay it in the bottom of a Gallipot, and then fill it with sugar, and tie it up close, when you have spent that sugar, put in some more, it will be well perfumed.

229. *An excellent way to make Syrup of Roses, or of any other Flower.*

Fill a Silver Bason three quarters full of Spring water, then fill it up with Rose-Leaves or any other, and cover it, and set it upon a pot of seething water one hour, then strain it, and put in more; and do in like manner, and so do seven times, then take to every Pint one Pound of Sugar, and make a Syrup therewith.

230. *To dry Rose Leaves.*

Pick your Roses, and dry them upon the Leads of a house in a Sun-shine day, and turn them as you do Hay, and when they are through dry, keep them in broadmouth'd Glasses close stopped.

231. *To Candy Flowers.*

Boil some Rosewater and Sugar together, then put in your Flowers being very dry and boil them a little, then strew in some fine Sugar over them, and turn them, and boil them a little more, then take them from the fire, and strew some more Sugar over them, then take them out and lay them to dry, and open them, and strew Sugar over them; they will dry in a few hours in a hot day.

232. *The making of Sugar-Plate and casting of it into Moulds.*

Take one Pound of double refin'd Sugar beaten and searced, and three Ounces of pure white Starch beaten and searced, then have some Gum-Dragon steeped in Rosewater, and put some of it with the Sugar and Starch and a little of Ambergreece into a Mortar, and beat them till they come to a perfect Paste, you must also put in a little White of an Egg with the Gum, then mould it with searced Sugar, then dust your Moulds with Sugar, then roul out your Paste and lay it into the Mould, pressing it down into every hollow part with your fingers, and when it hath taken impression, knock the Mould on the edge against a Table and it will come out, or you may help it with the point of your knife; if you find you have put in too much Gum, then add more Sugar, if too much Sugar, then more Gum, work it up as fast as you can, when they come out of the Moulds trim them handsomely; if you would make saucers, dishes, or bowls, you must rowl it out thin and put your Paste into a saucer, dish, or bowl for a Mould, and let them stand therein till they be very dry, then gild them on the edges with the white of and Egg laid round about the edge with a pencil, and press the Gold down with some Cotton, and when it is dry brush off the superfluous loose Gold with the foot of an Hare, and if you would have your Paste exceeding smooth, as for Cards or the like, then roul your Paste upon a slicked paper with a very smooth Rouling-pin; if you would colour any of it, you must take the searced powder of any Herbs or Flowers, first dryed, and put to it when you beat it in a Mortar with the Gum.

233. *To make Paste of Almonds.*

Take four Ounces of *Valentia* Almonds, blanched and beaten with Rosewater till it come to perfect Paste, then take stale white bread, grate it and sift it, and dry it by the fire, then put that to your Almonds with the weight of all in fine Sugar, beat them very well, and put in some Spice beaten and searced, then when it is a little cool, roul it out, dust your Moulds and print it, and dry it in an Oven, you may if you please put the juice of a Limon into it when it is beating, you may make some of it into Jumbolds, and tie them in knots and bake them upon Buttered Plates, and when they are baked, ice them over with Rosewater, Sugar, and the White of an Egg, and set them into the Oven again for a while.

234. *To make French Bisket.*

Take half a Peck of fine Flower, two Ounces of Coriander seeds, the Whites of four Eggs, half a Pint of Ale Yest, and as much water as will make it up into a stiff Paste, let your water be blood warm, then bake it in a long Roll as big as your Thigh, let it be in the Oven but one hour, when it is two days old, pare it and slice it thin over-thwart, then ice it over thin, and set it into the Oven to dry.

235. *To make Ginger-bread.*

Take three stale Manchets grated and sifted, then put to them half an Ounce of Cinamon, as much Ginger, half an Ounce of Licoras and Aniseeds together, beat all these and searce them, and put them in with half a Pound of fine Sugar, boil all these together with a quart of Claret, stirring them continually till it come to a stiff Paste, then when it is almost cold, mould it on a Table with some searced Spice and Sugar, then bake it in what shape you please.

236. *Another sort of Ginger-bread.*

Take half a pound of sweet Almonds blanched and beaten, half a pound of fine Flower first dried in an Oven, one Pound of fine Sugar, what sorts of Spices you please, beaten and searced, and also Seeds, beat all these together with two Eggs, both Yolks and Whites, then mould it with flower and Sugar together, and so bake it in what shape you please.

237. *To make Puff-Paste.*

Take a quart of the finest Flower, the Whites of three Eggs, and the Yolks of two, and a little cold water, make it into a perfect Paste, then roul it abroad thin, then lay on little bits of Butter, and fold it over again, then drive it abroad again, and lay on more Butter, and then fold it over, and so do ten times, make it up for your use, and put your Fruit or Meat therein and bake it.

238. *Another way for Puff-Paste.*

Take fine Flower half a Peck, the Yolks of five Eggs and one White, one Pound of Butter, half a pint of Cream, and a little fair water, break your Butter in little Bits and do not mould it too much, but roul it abroad so soon as you can, and let the Butter be seen in spots, for that will make it hollow when it comes into the Oven, then put in your Meat or Fruit, and close it over, and wash it over with the Yolk of an Egg and Cream beaten together, just when you set it into the Oven; let your Oven be quick, but do not let it stand too long, for that will spoil it.

239. *To make short Paste without Butter.*

Bake your Flower first, then take a quart of it, and the Yolks of three Eggs and a Pint of Cream, two Ounces of fine Sugar, and a little Salt, and so make it into Paste.

240. *To Candy whole Spices with a hard Rock-Candy.*

Take one Pound of fine Sugar, and eight spoonfuls of Rosewater, and the weight of six pence of Gum Arabick that is clear, boil them together till a drop will run as small as a hair; then put it into an earthen Pipkin, and having before steeped your spices one night or two in Rosewater, put your spices into the Pipkin, and stop it up close that no Air get in, keep it in a hot place three weeks, then break your Pot with a Hammer.

Thus you may do with preserved Oranges and Limons, any kinds of Fruits and flowers, or Herbs if you please.

241. *To make very fine Bisket.*

Take half a Pound of searced Sugar, the Yolks of six Eggs, a little searced spice and Seeds, and a little Ambergreece or Musk, your Eggs must be very hard, then put all these into a Mortar and beat them to a Paste with a little Gum Dragon steeped in Rosewater all night, then mould it up with fine Sugar; and make it into pretty Fancies, and dry them in a warm Oven.

242. *To make Orange, or Limon or Citron Bisket.*

Take either of these preserved and washed from their Syrup, beat them well in a Mortar, and then put in a little Gum Dragon as before, beat them again together till it be a perfect Paste, then mould it up with Sugar searced, and make them up in what shape you please and dry it.

243. *To make Bisket of Potato-Roots or Parsneps.*

Take their Roots boil'd very tender, and beat them in a Mortar with their weight of searced Sugar, then put in a little Gum dragon as before, beat them to a Paste, and mould them up with Sugar searced, and make them up in what shape you please, and dry them.

244. *To pickle Oranges or Limons, taught me by a Seaman.*

Take those which are free from any spots, and lay them gently in a Barrel, then fill up the Barrel with Sea-water, and so cover your Vessel close, for want of Sea-water, you may take fair water, and make it so strong with Bay Salt, that it will bear an Egg, and put to them in like manner.

245. *To keep Grapes fresh and green, taught me by a Sea-Captain.*

Take your fairest Grapes without any blemish, then lay some Oats in a Box; and then a Lay of Grapes, and then more Oats, and so do till you have laid all in, then cover the Grapes well with Oats, and close your box fast that no Air get in.

246. *To dry Grapes to keep longer.*

Take your best Clusters and hang them up in a Room upon Lines, and be sure you do not let them touch one another, they will keep four months.

247. *To make Marmalade of Oranges or Limons.*

Boil the Rinds of them in several Waters till they be very tender, beat them small with their weight of Pippins, then take the weight of all in fine Sugar, and to every Pound of Sugar, a Pint of Water, boil your Water and Sugar together, and make a Syrup, then put in your Pulp, and boil it a good while till it be clear, then put in the Juice of some Orange and Limon, so much as will give it a fine taste, then boil it a little longer till you see it will jelly very well, then put it into Glasses, and keep it in a reasonable warm place; this is very Cordial, and stoppeth Rheum.

248. *To make green Ginger wet.*

Take one pound of Ginger, and steep it in Red-Wine and Vinegar equally mixed, let it stand so close covered twelve days, and twice every day stir it up and down, then take two quarts of Red-Wine and as much Vinegar, and boil them together a little while, then put in three pounds of Sugar and make a Syrup therewith, then put in your Ginger and boil it a while, then set it by till the next day, so boil it every day a little, till it be very clear, and so keep it in the Syrup.

249. *To make a Sallad of Limons.*

Take the rinds of Limons cut in halves, and boil them in several waters till they are very tender, then take Vinegar, Water and Sugar, and make a Syrup, then put in your Limons, first cut as you would an Apple-paring, round and round till you come at the top, boil them a while in the Syrup, then set them by till the next day, then boil them again a little, and so do till you see they be clear, and the Syrup thick; when you serve them to the Table, wash them in Vinegar.

250. *To stew Prunes without fire.*

Take your largest Prunes well washed, and put them into a broad mouthed Glass, then put to them some Claret Wine, and whole Spice, and cover your Glass very well, and set it in the Sun ten days or more, and they will eat very finely; you must also put a little Sugar into the Glass with them.

251. *To make Syrup of the Juice of Citrons or Limons.*

Take the Juyce of either of them, and put twice the weight of fine Sugar therein, put it into a long Gallipot, and set that pot into a Kettle of boiling water, till you see they be well incorporated, then take it out, and when it is cold put it up.

252. *To make Punch.*

Take one Quart of Claret wine, half a Pint of Brandy, and a little Nutmeg grated, a little Sugar, and the Juice of a Limon, and so drink it.

253. *To make Limonado.*

Take one Quarrt of Sack, half a Pint of Brandy, half a Pint of fair Water, the Juyce of two Limons, and some of the Pill, so brew them together, with Sugar, and drink it.

254. *To make Paste of Pomewaters.*

Take your Pomewater Apples, and put them in a long Gallipot, and set that Pot in a Kettle of boiling water, till your Apples are tender, then pare them, and cut them from the Core, and beat them in a Mortar very well, then take their weight in fine Sugar, and boil it to a Candy height with a little water, then put in your Apples, and boil them till it will come from the bottom of the Posnet, when it is almost cold mould it with searced Sugar, and make it in Cakes and dry them.

255. *To make Syrup of Rasberries, or of other Fruits, as Grapes or the like.*

Take the Juyce of your Fruits and the weight thereof in fine Sugar, mix them together, and put them into a long Gally-pot, and set that pot into a Kettle of seething water, and when you see it is enough let it cool, and then put it up; after you have strained out your Juice, you must let it stand to settle three or four days before you put the Sugar into it, and then take only the clearest, this is exceeding good and comfortable in all Feavers.

256. *To make a Caudle for a sick body both pleasant and comfortable.*

Take a quart of white Wine, and boil it a while with a Blade of large Mace, and a little whole Cinamon, then take four Ounces of sweet Almonds blanched and beaten with a little Rosewater, then strain your Almonds with the Wine, and set it over the fire again, and when it is scalding hot, put in the Yolks of four Eggs, and as much Sugar as you think fit.

257. *How to cover all kinds of Seeds, or little pieces of Spices, or Orange or Limon Pill, with Sugar for Comfits.*

First of all you mast have a deep bottomed Basin of Brass or Latin, with two ears of Iron to hang it with two Cords over some hot Coals.

You must also have a broad Pan to put Ashes in, and hot Coals upon them.

You must have a Brass Ladle to let run the Sugar upon the Seeds.

You must have a Slice of Brass to scrape away the Sugar from the sides of the hanging Basin if need be.

Having all these things in readiness, do as followeth;

Take fine white Sugar beaten, and let your Seeds and Spice be dry, then dry them again in your hanging Basin:

Take to every two pounds of Sugar one quarter of a pound of Spices or Seeds, or such like.

If it be Aniseeds, two pounds of Sugar to half a pound of Aniseeds, will be enough.

Melt your Sugar in this manner, put in three Pounds of Sugar into the Basin, and one Pint of Water, stir it well till it be wet, then melt it very well and boil it very softly until it will stream from the Ladle like Turpentine, and not drop, then let it seeth no more, but keep it upon warm Embers, that it may run from the Ladle upon the seeds.

Move the Seeds in the hanging Basin so fast as you can or may, and with one hand, cast on half a Ladle full at a time of the hot Sugar, and rub the Seeds with your other hand a pretty while, for that will make them take the Sugar the better, and dry them well after every Coat.

Do thus at every Coat, not only in moving the Basin, but also with stirring of the Comfits with the one hand, and drying the same: in every hour you may make three pounds of Comfits; as the Comfits do increase in bigness, so you may take more Sugar in your Ladle to cast on:

But for plain Comfits, let your Sugar be of a light decoction last, and of a high decoction first, and not too hot.

For crisp and ragged Comfits make your decoction so high, as that it may run from the Ladle, and let it fall a foot high or more from the Ladle, and the hotter you cast on your sugar, the more ragged will your Comfits be; also the Comfits will not take so much of the sugar, as upon a light decoction, and they will keep their raggedness long; this high decoction must serve for eight or ten Coats, and put on at every time but one Ladle full.

A quarter of a pound of Coriander seeds, and three pounds of sugar, will serve for very great Comfits.

See that you keep your Sugar in the Basin always in good temper, that it burn not in Lumps, and if at any time it be too high boiled, put in a spoonful or two of water, and keep it warily with your Ladle, and let your fire be always very clear, when your Comfits be made, set them in Dishes upon Paper in the Sun or before the Fire, or in the Oven after Bread is drawn, for the space of one hour or two, and that will make them look very white.

257. [Transcriber's note: so numbered in original] *To make a fine Cullis or Jelly.*

Take a red Cock, scald, wash, and dress him clean, seeth it in white Wine or Rhenish Wine, and scum it clean, put in a Pint of thick cream to it, then put in whole Spices, Sugar and Rosewater, and boil them together.

258. *A white Jelly with Almonds.*

Take Rosewater and Gum Dragon first steeped, or Isinglass dissolved, and some Cinamon whole, seeth these together, then take one pound of Almond blanched and beaten with Rosewater, then put them in and seeth them with the rest, stir them always, and when it is enough, sweeten it to your taste, and when it is cold eat it.

259. *To make sweet Cakes without Sugar.*

Wash some Parsnep roots, scrape them and slice them very thin dry them in a Dish in an Oven, and beat them to a Powder, mix them with an equal quantity of fine Flower, mix them with Cream, beaten Spice and Salt, and so make them and bake them.

260. *To keep Roses or Gilliflowers very long.*

Take them when they are very fresh, and in the bud, and gathered very dry, dip them in the whites of Eggs well beaten, and presently strew thereon searced sugar, and put them up in luted Pots, and set them in a cool place, in sand or gravel, and with a Filip of your finger at any time you may strike off the coat, and you will have the Flower fresh and fair.

261. *How to keep Walnuts long fresh and good.*

Make a lay of the dry stampings of Crabs when the Verjuice is pressed forth, then a Lay of Walnuts, and then Crabs again, till all be in, then cover the Vessel very well, and when you eat them, they will be as though they were new gathered.

262. *To pickle Quinces.*

Put them into a Vessel, and fill up the Vessel with small Ale, or white Wine Lees, which is better, and cover your Vessel well that no Air get in.

263. *To keep Artichokes.*

Take your Artichokes, and cut off the stalks within two inches of the Apple, and of these stalks make a strong Decoction, slicing them into thin and small pieces, and boil them with water and salt; when it is cold, put in your Artichokes, and keep them from the Air.

When you spend them, lay them first in warm water, and then in cold, to take away the bitterness.

264. *To make Clove or Cinamon Sugar.*

Put Sugar in a Box, and lay Spices among it, and close up the Box fast, and in short time it will smell and tast very well.

265. *To make Irish* Aquavitæ.

Take to every Gallon of good *Aquavitæ*, two Ounces of Licoras bruised, two ounces of Aniseeds bruised, let them stand six days in a Vessel of Glass close stopped, then pour out as much of it as will run clear, dissolve in that clear six great spoonfuls of the best Molasses, then put it into another Glass, then add to it some Dates and Raisins of the Sun stoned; this is very good for the Stomach.

266. *To distil Roses speedily.*

Stamp your Roses in a Mortar with a little Rosewater, and then distill them: This way will yield more water by much than the common way.

267. *To make Scotch Brewis.*

Take a Manchet and pare off the crust then slice it thin and whole round the Loaf, and lay these slices into a deep dish cross ways, one slice lying upon the edge of the other a little, that they may lye quite cross the dish, then fill it up with Cream and put whole Spice therein, so set it over a Chafing-dish of Coals very hot, and always cast the Cream all over the Bread with a spoon till all be spent, which will be above an hour, then take some Sack and sweeten it with Sugar, and pour all over it, and serve it to the Table.

268. *To make fine Black Puddings.*

Take the Blood of a Hog, and strain it, and let it stand to settle, putting in a little Salt while it is warm, then pour off the water on the top of the Blood, and put so much Oatmeal as you think fit, let it stand all night, then put in eight Eggs beaten very well, as much Cream as you think fit, one Nutmeg or more grated, some Pennyroyal and other Herbs shred small, good store of Beef Sewet shred very small, and a little more Salt, mix these very well together, and then have your Guts very well scoured, and scraped with the back of a Knife, fill them but not too full, then when you have tyed them fast, wash them in fair water, and let your water boil when they go in; then boil them half an hour, then stir them with the handle of a Ladle and take them up and lay them upon clean straw, and prick them with a Needle, and when they are a little cool put them into the boiling water again, and boil them till they are enough.

269. *To make the best Almond-Puddings.*

Take a quart of thick Cream and boil it a while with whole Spice, then put in half a pound of sweet Almonds blanched and beaten to a Paste with Rosewater, boil these together till it will come from the bottom of the Posnet, continually stirring it for fear it burn:

Then put it out, and when it is cool, put in twelve yolks of Eggs, and six Whites, some Marrow in big Bits, or Beef Suet shred small, as much Sugar as you think fit, then fill your Guts being clean scraped; you may colour some of them if you please, and into some put plumped Currans, and boil them just as you do the other.

270. *To make a Rice pudding to bake.*

Take three Pints of Milk or more, and put therein a quarter of a Pound of Rice, clean washed and picked, then set them over the fire, and let them warm together, and often stir them with a wooden Spoon, because that will not scrape too hard at the bottom, to make it burn, then let it boil till it be very thick, then take it off and let it cool, then put in a little Salt, some beaten Spice, some Raisins and Currans, and some Marrow, or Beef Suet shred very small, then butter your Pan, and so bake it, but not too much.

271. *To make a Pudding of wild Curds.*

Take wild Curds and Cream with them, put thereto Eggs, both yolks and whites, Rosewater, Sugar, and beaten Spice with some Raisins and Currans, and some Marrow, and a little Salt, then butter a Pan, and bake it.

272. *To make Pudding of Plum Cake.*

Slice your Cake into some Cream or Milk, and boil it, and when it is cold, put in Eggs, Sugar, a little Salt and some Marrow, so butter a Pan and bake it, or fill guts with it.

273. *To make Bisket Pudding.*

Take Naples Biskets and cut them into Milk, and boil it, then put in Eggs, Spice Sugar, Marrow, and a little Salt, and so boil it and bake it.

274. *To make a dry Oatmeal Pudding.*

Take your Oatmeal well picked, and put into it a little Salt, some Raisins and Currans, and some beaten spice, and good store of Beef Suet finely shred, so tie it up hard in a Cloth, and let your water boil when you put it in; and let it boil very well; if you would butter it, then leave out the Suet; and if you would leave out the Fruit, then put in sweet herbs good store.

275. *To make Almond puddings a different way from the other.*

Take two Manchets and grate them, then scald them in some Cream, then put in some Almonds Blanched and beaten as you do other, with Rosewater, let there be about half a pound, then put in eight Eggs well beaten, some Spice, Sugar, Salt and Marrow, and having your Guts well scowred and scraped, fill them, but not too full, and boil them as you do the other; or bake it if you please; Currans will do well in it.

276. *To make a Quaking Pudding.*

Take Grated Bread, a little Flower, Sugar, Salt, beaten Spice, and store of Eggs well beaten, mix these well, and beat them together, then dip a clean

Cloth in hot water, and flower it over, and let one hold it at the four corners till you put it in, so tie it up hard, and let your Water boil when you put it in, then boil it for one hour, and serve it in with Sack, Sugar and Butter.

277. *To make good Dumplings.*

Take some Flower and a little Salt, and a little Ale-Yest, and so much water as will make it into a Paste, so let your water boil when you do put them in; boil them but a little while, and then butter them.

278. *Another way to make Dumplings.*

Take half a quarter of a Peck of Flower, and one Egg, yolk and white, half a Pound of Butter broke in little Bits, mix them together with so much cold Milk as will make it up, do not break your Butter too small, for then they will not flake; make them up like Rouls of Butter, and when your water boils, put them in, and do not boil them too much, then butter them.

279. *Another way to make Dumplings.*

Take Flower and temper it very light with Eggs, Milk, or rather Cream, beaten Spice, Salt, and a little Sugar, then wet a Cloth in hot water, and flower it, and so boil it for a Pudding, or else make it pretty stiff with the Flower and a little grated Bread, and so boil them for Dumplings, then butter them, and serve them in.

280. *To make a green Pudding to Butter.*

Take a Quart of Cream and boil it, then put in twelve Eggs, yolks and whites well beaten, and one Manchet grated small, a little salt, beaten Spice and some Sugar:

Then colour it well with some Juice of Spinage, or if you will have it yellow, colour it with Saffron, so boil it in a wet Cloth flowred as before, and serve it in with Wine, Sugar and Butter, and stick it with blanched Almonds split in halves, and pour the sauce over it, and it will look like a Hedghog.

You may at some time stick it with Candied Orange Pill or Limon Pill, or Eringo Roots Candied, you may sometimes strew on some Caraway Comfits, and if you will bake it, then put in some Marrow, and some Dates cut small: thus you have many Puddings taught in one.

281. *To make a Pudding of a Hogs Liver.*

Take your liver and boil it in water and salt, but not too much;

Then beat it fine in a Mortar, and put to it one Quart of Cream, a little Salt, Rosewater, Sugar, beaten Spice and Currans, with six Eggs beaten very well: mix it well.

And if you bake it, put in Marrow, or if you boil it in Skins.

But if you boil it in a Cloth, then leave it out; and butter it when it is boiled.

282. *To make a Rasberry Pudding.*

Take a Quart of Cream and boil it with whole Spice a while, then put in some grated Bread, and cover it off the Fire, that it may scald a little; then put in eight Eggs well beaten, and sweeten it with Sugar; then put in a Pint or more of whole Rasberries, and so boil it in a Cloth, and take heed you do not boil it too much, then serve it in with Wine, Butter and Sugar.

You may sometimes leave out the Rasberries, and put in Cowslip Flowers, or Goosberries.

283. *To make a Calves foot Pudding.*

Take those which are tenderly boiled and shred them small with Beef-Suet, then put to four Feet one quart of Cream and eight Eggs well beaten, a little Salt, some Rosewater and Sugar, some beaten Spice, and one pound of Currans; mix all these well together, and boil it or bake it; but if you would Butter it, then do not put in Suet.

284. *To make a Pudding to rost.*

Take a Pint of Cream, scald a little grated Bread in it, then put in three Eggs beaten, a little Flower, Currans, beaten Spice, Suet, Sugar and Salt, with some Beef Suet finely shred, make it pretty stiff, and wrap it in a Lambs Caul, and rost it on a Spit with a Loin of Lamb; if you please, you may put in a little Rosewater.

285. *To make Cream of divers things.*

Take a Quart of Cream and boil it a while, then put in eight yolks of Eggs, and six Whites well beaten, put them in over the Fire, and stir them lest they turn, then when it is almost enough, put in some Candied Eringo Root, Orange or Limon Pill Candied, and cut thin, preserved Plums, without the Stones, Quince, Pippin, Cherries, or the like; if you do not like it so thick, put fewer Eggs into it.

286. *To make Cream of Artichoke Bottoms.*

Take a Quart of Cream and boil it with a little whole Mace a while; then have your Artichoke Bottoms boiled very tender, and bruise them well in a Mortar, then put them into the Cream, and boil them a while, then put in so many yolks of Eggs as you think fit, and sweeten it to your taste; when you think it is enough, pour it out, and serve it in cold.

287. *To pickle Barberries.*

Take your Barberries and pick out the fairest Bunches of them, then take the Refuse, and with some Water and Salt, so strong as will bear an Egg, boil them together for half an hour or more, then lay your fair Bunches into a Pot, and when the Liquor is cold, pour it over them.

288. *To pickle French Beans.*

Take them before they be too old, and boil them tender, then put them into a pickle made with Vinegar and Salt, and so keep them; it is a very good and pleasant Sallad.

289. *To pickle Oysters.*

Take your great Oysters, and in opening them save the Liquor, then strain it from dross, add to it some White Wine, and White Wine Vinegar, and a little Salt, and so let them boil together a while, putting in whole Mace, whole Cloves, whole Pepper, sliced Ginger, and quartered Nutmegs, with a few Bay leaves; when the Liquor is boiled almost enough, put in your Oysters and plump them, then lay them out to cool, then put them into a

Gally-pot or Barrel, and when the Liquor is cool, pour it over them, and keep them from the Air.

290. *To make the best sort of Mustard.*

Dry your Seed very well, then beat it by little and little at a time in a Mortar, and sift it, then put the Powder into a Gally-pot, and wet it with Vinegar very well, then put in a whole Onion, pilled but not cut, a little Pepper beaten, a little Salt, and a lump of stone Sugar.

291. *Another sort of Mustard.*

Dry your Horse-Radish Roots in an Oven very dry, then beat them to Powder and sift them, and when you would use any, wet it with Wine Vinegar, and so it will rather be better than the other.

292. *To keep boiled powdered Beef long after it is boiled.*

When your Beef is well powdered, and boiled thorowly, and quite cold, wrap it up close in a linnen cloth, and then a woollen one, and so keep it in a Chest or Box from the Air.

293. *To make Clouted Cream.*

Take three Gallons of new Milk, set it on the fire, and boil it, then put in two Quarts of Cream, and stir it about for a while over the fire, then pour it out into several pans, and cover it till the next morning, then take it off carefully with a Skimmer, and put it all into one dish one upon another, then eat it with Wine and Sugar.

THE

Queen-like CLOSET,

OR

Rich Cabinet.

THE SECOND PART.

1. *To make Elder Vinegar and to colour it.*

Take of your best white Wine Vinegar, and put such a quantity of ripe Elder Berries into it as you shall think fit, in a wide mouth'd Glass, stop it close, and set it in the Sun for about ten days, then pour it out gently into another Glass, and keep it for your use; thus you may make Vinegar of Red Roses, Cowslipps, Gilliflowers, or the like.

2. *To make Metheglin, either Brown or White, but White is best.*

Take what quantity you please of Spring-Water, and make it so strong with Honey that it will bear an Egg, then boil it very well, till a good part be wasted, and put in to it boiling a good quantity of whole Spice, Rosemary, Balm, and other cordial and pleasant Herbs or Flowers.

When it is very well boiled, set it to cool, it being strained from the Herbs, and the Bag of Spices taken out;

When it is almost cold, put in a little Yest, and beat it well, then put it into Vessels when it is quite cold, and also the Bag of Spice, and when it hath stood a few days, bottle it up; if you would have it red, you must put the Honey to strong Ale Wort in stead of Water.

3. *To make Collar'd Beef.*

Take a good Flank of Beef, and lay it in Pump water and Salt, or rather Saltpeter, one day and one night, then take Pepper, Mace, Nutmegs, Ginger, and Cloves, with a little of the Herb called Tarragon, beat your Spice, shred your Tarragon, and mingle these with some Suet beaten small, and strew upon your Beef, and so rowl it up, and tie it hard, and bake it in a pot with Claret Wine and Butter, let the pot be covered close, and something in the pot to keep the Meat down in the Liquor that it may not scorch, set it into the Oven with Houshold bread, and when it is baked, take it out, and let it cool, then hang it up one night in the Chimney before you eat it, and so as long as you please.

Serve it in with Bay Leaves, and eat it with Mustard and Sugar.

4. *To make Almond Puddings with French Rolls or Naples Biskets.*

Take a Quart of Cream, boil it with whole Spice, then take it from the Fire, and put in three Naples Biskets, or one Penny French Roll sliced thin, and cover it up to scald; when it is cold, put in four Ounces of sweet Almonds blanched, and beaten with Rosewater, the Yolks of eight Eggs, and a little Marrow, with as much Sugar as you think fit, and a little Salt;

you may boil it, or bake it, or put it into Skins; if it be boiled or baked, put Sugar on it when you serve it in.

5. *To make Barley Cream.*

Take two Ounces of French Barley, and boil it in several Waters, then take a quart of Cream, and boil it with whole Spice, put in your Barley, and boil them together very well,

Then put in the yolks of six Eggs well beaten, and as much Sugar as you think fit; stir them well over the fire, then poure it out, and when it is cold serve it in; thus you may make Rice Cream, onely do not boil that, but a very little in Milk, before you put it into the Cream.

6. *To make Cheese-cakes.*

Take four Gallons of new Milk, set it with a little Runnet, and when it is come, break it gently, and whey it very well, then take some Manchet, first scalded well in new Milk, let the Milk be thick with it, and while it is hot, put in a quarter of a pound of fresh Butter, and stir it in, when it is cold, mix that and your curd together very well, then put in one Pound and half of plumped Currans, some beaten Spice, a very little Salt, Rosewater, and the yolks of eight Eggs, half a Pint of Cream, and a little Sugar, mix them well together, then make some Paste, with Flower, Butter, the yolk of an Egg and fair water, and roul it out thin, and so bake them in bake-pans, and do not let them stand too long in the Oven.

7. *Another way for Cheese-cakes.*

Take the Curd of four Gallons of new Milk, and put thereto half a pound of Almonds blanched and beaten fine with Rosewater, then put in one Pint of Raw Cream, the yolks of ten Eggs, some beaten Spice, a little Salt, one pound and half of plumped Currans, a little Rosewater, and some Sugar, and so mix them very well, and put them into your Crust and bake them.

8. *Another way for Cheese-cakes.*

Take the Curd of four Gallons of new Milk, beat it well in a Mortar with half a pound of fresh Butter, and then season it as you do the other above-named.

9. *Another way for Cheese-cakes.*

Take the same quantity of Curd, and mix it with half a Pound of Rice boiled tender in Milk, one quarter of a pound of fresh Butter, the yolks of eight Eggs, one Pint of Cream, beaten Spice, two pounds of Currans first plumped, Rosewater and Sugar, and a little Salt, and so bake them, not too much.

10. *To make fresh Cheese.*

Take some very tender Cheese-Curd, stamp it very well in a Mortar with a little Rosewater, wherein whole Spice hath been steeped, then let it stand in a little Cullender about half an hour, then turn it out into your Dish, and serve it to the Table with Cream, Wine, and Sugar.

11. *Another way for a fresh Cheese.*

Take a quart of Cream, and boil in it whole Spice, then stir in the yolks of eight Eggs, and four whites well beaten, and when they are hot, put in so much Sack as will give it a good taste, then stir it over the Fire till it runneth on a Curd, then beat it in a Mortar as the other, and serve it to the Table with Cream and Sugar.

12. *To make Oatmeal Pudding.*

Take Oatmeal beaten fine, put to it some Cream, beaten Spice, Rosewater and Sugar, some Currans, some Marrow, or Beef Suet shred fine, and a little Salt, then Butter your pan and bake it.

13. *Puddings in Balls to stew or to fry.*

Take part of a Leg of Veal, parboil it, and shred it fine with some Beef Suet, then take some Cream, Currans, Spice, Rosewater, Sugar and a little Salt, a little grated Bread, and one handful of Flower, and with the yolks of Eggs make them in Balls, and stew them between two Dishes, with Wine and Butter, or you may make some of them in the shape of Sausages, and fry them in Butter, so serve them to the Table with Sugar strewed over them.

14. *To boil Pigeons.*

Take your largest Pigeons and cut them in halves, wash them and dry them, then boil a little water and Salt with some whole Spice, and a little Faggot of sweet Herbs, then put in your Pigeons and boil them, and when they are enough, take some boiled Parsley shred small, some sweet Butter, Claret Wine, and an Anchovy, heat them together, then put in the yolks of Eggs, and make it thick over the Fire, then put in your Pigeons into a Dish, garnished with pickled Barberries and raw Parsley, and so pour over them your Sawce, and serve it to the Table.

15. *To make an Apple Tansie.*

Take a Quart of Cream, one Manchet grated, the yolks of ten Eggs, and four Whites, a little Salt, some Sugar, and a little Spice, then cut your Apples in round thin slices, and lay them into your Frying-Pan in order, your Batter being hot, when your Apples are fried, pour in your Butter, and fry it on the one side, then turn it on a Pie-Plate and slide it into the Pan again, and fry it, then put it on a Pie-Plate, and squeez the Juice of a Limon over it, and strew on fine Sugar, and serve it so to the Table.

16. *To make a green Tansie to fry, or boil over a Pot.*

Take a Quart of Cream, the yolks of one dozen of Eggs and half, their Whites well beat, mix them together, and put in one Nutmeg grated, then colour it well with the Juice of Spinage, and sweeten it with Sugar; then fry it with Butter as you do the other, and serve it in the same manner; but you must lay thin slices of Limon upon this.

If you will not fry it, then butter a Dish, and pour it therein, and set it upon a Pot of boiling water till it be enough; this is the better and easier way.

Thus you may make Tansies of any other things, as Cowslips, Rasberries, Violets, Marigolds, Gilliflowers, or any such like, and colour them with their Juice; you may use green Wheat instead of Spinage.

17. *To make an Amulet.*

Take twelve Eggs, beat them and strain them, put to them three or four spoonfuls of Cream, then put in a little Salt, and having your frying-pan ready with some Butter very hot, pour it in, and when you have fryed it a little, turn over both the sides into the middle, then turn it on the other side, and when it is fryed, serve it to the table with Verjuice, Butter and Sugar.

18. *To make a Chicken-Pie.*

Make your Paste with cold Cream, Flower, Butter and the yolk of an Egg, roul it very thin, and lay it in your Baking-pan, then lay Butter in the Bottom.

Then lay in your Chickens cut in quarters with some whole Mace, and Nutmeg sliced, with some Marrow, hard Lettuce, Eryngo Root, and Citron Pill, with a few Dates stoned and sliced:

Then lay good store of Butter, Close up your Pie and Bake it:

Then Cut it open, and put in some Wine, Butter, and Sugar with the Yolks of two or three Eggs well beaten together over the fire, till it be thick, so serve it to the Table, and garnish your Dish with some pretty Conceits made in Paste.

19. *To make a Collar of Brawn of a Breast of Pork.*

Take a large Breast of Pork, and bone it, then roul it up, and tie it hard with a Tape, then boil it water and Salt till it be very tender, then make Souce drink for it with small Beer, Water and Salt, and keep it in it:

Serve it to the Table with a Rosemary Branch in the middle of it, and eat it with Mustard.

20. *To souce Veal to eat like Sturgeon.*

Take what part of Veal you like best, and boil it with water and salt, and a bundle of sweet herbs, and a little Limon Pill; when it is boiled enough, put into your Liquor so much Vinegar as will make it tast sharp, and a Limon sliced, and when it is cold, put in your Veal, and when it hath lain four or five days, serve it to the Table with Fennel, and eat it with some Vinegar; you must tie it up as you do Brawn.

21. *To make a Pasty of a Breast of Veal.*

Take half a peck of fine Flower, and two pounds of Butter broken into little bits, one Egg, a little Salt, and as much cold Cream, or Milk as will make it into a Paste; when you have framed your Pasty, lay in your Breast of Veal boned, and seasoned with a little Pepper and Salt, but first you must lay in Butter.

When your Veal is laid in, then put in some large Mace, and a Limon sliced thin, Rind and all, then cover it well with Butter, close it and bake it, and when you serve it in, cut it up while it is very hot, put in some white wine, sugar, the yolks of Eggs, and Butter being first heated over the Fire together; this is very excellent meat.

22. *To make a Pigeon-Pie.*

Make your Paste as for the Pasty, roul it thin, and lay it into your baking-pan, then lay in Butter, then mix Pepper and Salt and Butter together, and fill the bellies of your Pigeons, then lay them in, and put in some large Mace, and little thin slices of Bacon, then cover them with Butter, and close your Pie, and bake it not too much.

23. *To boil a Capon or Hen with Oysters.*

Take either of them, and fill the Belly of it with Oysters, and truss it, then boil it in white Wine, Water, the Liquor of the Oysters, a Blade or two of Mace, a little Pepper whole, and a little Salt; when it is boiled enough, take the Oysters out of the belly, and put them into a Dish, then take some Butter, and some of the Liquor it was boiled in, and two Anchoves with the yolks of Eggs well beaten, heat these together over the fire, and then put your Oysters into it, then garnish your Dish with Limon sliced thin, and some of the Oysters, also some pickled Barberries and raw Parsley, then lay your Capon or Hen in the middle of it, and pour the sauce upon the Breast of it, then lay on sliced Limon and serve it in.

24. *To make an Olio.*

First lay in your Dish a Fricasy made of a Calves-head, with Oisters and Anchovies in it, then lay Marrow-bones round the Dish, within them lay Pigeons boiled round the Dish, and thin slices of Bacon, lay in the middle upon your Fricasy a powdred Goose boiled, then lay some sweet-breads of Veal fryed, and balls of Sawsage-meat here and there, with some Scotch Collops of Veal or of Mutton: Garnish your Dish with Limon or Orange and some toasts for the Marrow so serve it in.

25. *To make Cracknels.*

Take half a Pound of fine Flower, and as much fine Sugar, a few Coriander seeds bruised, and some Butter rubbed into the Flower, wet it with Eggs, Rosewater and Cream, make it into a Paste, and rowl it in thin Cakes, then prick them and bake them; then wash them over with Egg and a little Rosewater, then dry them again in the Oven to make them crisp.

26. *To make good Sauce for a boiled Leg of Mutton.*

Take the best Prunes and stew them well with white Wine or Claret, and some whole Spice, then drain them into a Dish and set it over a Chafing dish of Coles; put to it a little grated Bread, juice of Limon and a little salt, then lay your Mutton in a Dish, being well boiled with water and salt, pour your sauce to it:

Garnish your Dish with Limon, Barberries, Parsly, and so serve it in.

27. *To rost Pork without the Skin.*

Take any joint of small Pork, not salted and lay it to the fire till the Skin may be taken off, then take it from the fire and take off the Skin, then stick it with Rosemary and Cloves, and lay it to the fire again, then salt it and rost it carefully, then make Sauce for it with Claret Wine, white bread sliced thin, a little water, and some beaten Cinamon; boil these well together, then put in some Salt, a little Butter, Vinegar, or Juice of Limon, and a little sugar, when your Pork is rosted enough, then flower it, and lay it into a Dish with the Sauce, and serve it in.

28. *To roste a Pig like Lamb.*

Take a Pig—cut it in quarters, and truss it like quarters of Lamb, then spit it, and rost it till you may take off the Skin, then take the Spit from the fire, and take the skin clean off, then draw it with Parsly, and lay it to the fire, baste it with Butter, and when it is enough, flower it and serve it to the Table with Butter, the Juice of Orange, and gross Pepper, and a little Salt.

Take your largest Cucumbers, and wash them and put them into boiling water made quick with Salt, then when they are boiled enough, take them and peel them and break them into a Cullender, and when the Water is well drained from them, put them into a hot Dish, and pour over them some Butter and Vinegar a little Pepper and Salt, strew Salt on your Dish brims, lay some of the Rind of them about the Dish cut in several Fancies, and so serve them to the Table.

45. *To make several Sallads, and all very good.*

Take either the stalks of Mallows, or Turnip stalks when they run to seed, or stalks of the herb Mercury with the seedy head, either of these while they are tender put into boiling Water and Salt, and boiled tender, and then Butter and Vinegar over them.

46. *To make a Sallad of Burdock, good for the Stone, another of the tender stalks of Sow-thistles.*

Take the inside of the Stalks of Burdock, and cut them in thin slices, and lay them in water one whole day, shifting them sometimes, then boil them, and butter them as you do the forenamed.

Also the tender Stalks of Sow-thistles done in like manner, are very good and wholsome.

47. *To make a Tart of Spinage.*

Take a good quantity of green Spinage, boil it in water and salt, and drain it well in a Cullender, then put to it plumped Currans, Nutmeg, Salt, Sugar and Butter, with a little Cream, and the yolks of hard Eggs beaten fine, then having your Paste ready laid in your baking-pan, lay in a little butter, and then your Spinage, and then a little Butter again; so close it, and bake it, and serve it to the Table hot, with Sugar strewed over it.

48. *Artichoke Cream.*

Take the tender bottoms of Artichokes, and beat them in a Mortar, and pick out all the strings, then boil a quart of Cream with large Mace and Nutmeg, then put in your bottoms, and when they have boiled a while, put in the yolks of six Eggs well beaten, and so much Sugar as you think fit, and heat them together over the fire, then pour it into a Dish, and when it is cold serve it in with Sugar strewed over it.

49. *To make very fine Rolls for Noble Tables.*

Take half a Peck of fine Flower, the yolks of 4 Eggs and a little Salt, with a Pint of Ale yest, mix them together, and make them into a Paste with warm Milk and a little Sack, them mould it well, and put it into a warm Cloth to rise, when your Oven is hot, mould it again, and make it into little Rolls, and bake them, then rasp them, and put them into the Oven again for a while, and they will eat very crisp and fine.

50. *To make short Rolls.*

Take half a peck of fine Flower, and break into it one pound and half of fresh Butter very small, then bruised Coriander seeds, and beaten Spice with a very little Salt and some Sugar, and a Pint of Ale-yest, mix them well together, and make them into a Paste with warm Milk and Sack:

Then lay into it a warm Cloth to rise, and when your Oven is hot, make it into Rolls, and prick them, and bake them, and when they are baked, draw them and cover them till they be cold; these also eat very finely, if you butter some of them while they are hot.

51. *To dress Soals a fine way.*

Take one pair of your largest Soals, and flay them on both sides, then fry them in sweet Suet tried up with Spice, Bay leaves, and Salt, then lay them into a Dish, and put into them some Butter, Claret Wine and two Anchovies, cover them with another Dish, and set them over a Chafingdish of Coals, and let them stew a while, then serve them to the Table, garnish your Dish with Orange or Limon, and squeeze some over them.

52. *To stew Fish in the Oven.*

Take Soals, Whitings or Flounders, and put them into a Stew-pan with so much water as will cover them, with a little Spice and Salt, a little white Wine or Claret, some Butter, two Anchovies, and a bundle of sweet herbs, cover them and set them into an Oven not too hot; when they are enough, serve them in; Garnish your Dish wherein they lie with Barberries, raw Parsley, and slices of Limon, and lay Sippets in the bottom.

53. *To bake Collops of Bacon and Eggs.*

Take a Dish and lay a Pie-plate therein, then lay in your Collops of Bacon, and break your Eggs upon them.

Then lay on Parsley, and set them into an Oven not too hot, and they will be rather better than fried.

54. *To make Furmity.*

Take some new Milk or Cream, and boil it with whole Spice, then put in your Wheat or Pearl Barley boiled very tender in several Waters, when it hath boiled a while, thicken it with the yolks of Eggs well beaten, and sweeten it with Sugar, then serve it in with fine Sugar on the Brims of the Dish.

55. *To make Barly Broth.*

Take French Barley boiled in several waters, and to a Pound of it, put three quarts of water, boil them together a while with some whole Spice, then put in as many Raisins of the Sun and Currans as you think fit, when it is well boiled, put in Rosewater, Butter and Sugar, and so eat it.

56. *To make Barley Broth with Meat.*

Take a Knuckle of Veal, and the Crag-end of a Neck of Mutton, and boil them in water and salt, then put in some Barly, and whole Spice, and boil them very well together, then put in Raisins stoned, and Currans, and a few Dates stoned and sliced thin; when it is almost enough, put in some Cream, and boil it a while, then put in plumped Prunes, and the yolks of Eggs, Rosewater and Sugar, and a little Sack, so serve it in; Garnsh your Dish with some of the Raisins and Prunes and fine Sugar; this is very good and nourishing for sick or weak people.

57. *To make Furmity with Meat-Broth.*

Boil a Leg of Beef in water and salt, and put in a little whole Spice; when it is boiled tender; take it up, and put into the Broth some Wheat ready boiled, such as they sell in the Market, and when that hath boiled a while, put in some Milk, and let that boil a while, then thicken it with a little Flower, or the yolks of Eggs, then sweeten it with Sugar, and eat it.

58. *To make Furmity with Almonds.*

Take three Quarts of Cream, and boil it with whole Spice, then put in some pearled Barley first boiled in several waters, and when they have boiled together a while, then put in so many blanched Almonds beaten fine with Rosewater, as you think may be enough, about four Ounces of Barly to this quantity of Cream will be enough, and four Ounces of Almonds, boil them well together, and sweeten it with Sugar, and so serve it in, or eat it by the way, you may put in Saffron if you please.

59. *To make a hasty Pudding.*

Take one quart of Cream and boil it, then put in two Manchets grated, and one pound almost of Currans plumped, a little Salt, Nutmeg and Sugar, and a little Rosewater, and so let them boil together, stirring them continually over the Fire, till you see the butter arise from the Cream, and then pour it into a Dish and serve it in with fine Sugar strewed on the brims of the Dish.

60. *Another way to make a hasty Pudding.*

Take good new milk and boil it, then put in Flower, plumped Currans, beaten spice, Salt and Sugar, and stir it continually till you find it be enough, then serve it in with Butter and Sugar, and a little Wine if you please.

61. *To make Spanish Pap.*

Boil a quart of Cream with a little whole Spice, when it is well boiled, take out the Spice, and thicken it with Rice Flower, and when it is well boiled, put in the yolks of Eggs, and Sugar and Rosewater, with a very little Salt, so serve it to the Table either hot or cold, with fine Sugar strewed on the brims of the Dish.

62. *To make Gravie Broth.*

Take a good fleshy piece of Beef, not fat, and lay it down to the fire, and when it begins to rost, slash it with a Knife to let the Gravie run out, and continually bast it with what drops from it and Claret Wine mixed together, and continually cut it, and bast it till all the Gravie be out, then take this Gravie and set it over a Chafingdish of Coals with some whole Spice, Limon Pill, and a little Salt, when you think it is enough, lay some Sippets into another Dish, and pour it in, and serve it to the Table; Garnish your Dish with Limon and Orange; if you please you may leave out the Sippets and put in some poach'd Eggs, done carefully.

63. *To make French Pottage.*

Take an equal quantity of Chervil, hard Lettice and Sorrel, or any other Herb as you like best, in all as much as a Peck will hold pressed down, pick them well, and wash them, and drain them from the water, then put them into a Pot with half a pound of fresh Butter, and set them over the fire, and as the Butter melts, stir them down in it till they are all within the Butter, then put some water in, and a Crust of bread, with some whole Cloves and a little Salt, and when it is well boiled, take out the Crust of bread, and put in the yolks of four Eggs well beaten, and stir them together over the fire, then lay some thin slices of white bread into a deep dish, and pour it in.

64. *To make Cabbage Pottage.*

Take a Leg of Beef and a Neck of Mutton, and boil them well in water and salt, then put in good store of Cabbage cut small, and some whole Spice, and when it is boiled enough, serve it in.

65. *To make a Sallad of cold meat.*

Take the brawn of a cold Capon, or a piece of cold Veal, and mince it very small, with some Limon pill, then put in some Oil, Vinegar, Capers, Caviare, and some Anchovies, and mix them very well, then lay it in a Dish in the form of a Star, and serve it in; Garnish your Dish with Anchovies, Limon and Capers.

66. *To dry a Goose.*

Take a fair fat Goose, and powder it about a Month or thereabouts, then hang it up in a Chimney as you do Bacon, and when it is throughly dry, boil it well and serve it to the Table with some Mustard and Sugar, Garnish your Dish with Bay leaves: Hogs Cheeks are very good dried thus.

67. *To dress Sheeps Tongues with Oysters.*

Take your Sheeps Tongues about six of them, and boil them in water and salt till they be tender, then peel them, and slice them thin, then put them into a Dish with a quart of great Oisters; a little Claret wine and some whole Spice, let them stew together a while, then put in some Butter and the yolks of three Eggs well beaten, shake them well together, then lay some Sippets into a Dish, and put your Tongues upon them; Garnish your Dish with Oisters, Barberries, and raw Parsley, and serve it in.

68. *To make a Neats-tongue Pie.*

Let two small Neats tongues or one great one be tenderly boiled, then peel them and slice them very thin, season them with Pepper and Salt, and Nutmeg; then having your Paste ready laid into your baking-pan, lay some Butter in the bottom, then lay in your Tongues, and one pound of Raisins of the Sun, with a very little Sugar, then lay in more butter, so close it and bake it, then cut it up, and put in the yolks of three Eggs, a little Claret Wine and Butter, stir it well together, and lay on the Cover, and serve it; you may add a little Sugar if you please.

69. *A Capon with white Broth.*

Take a large Capon, and draw him, and truss him, and boil him in water and a little salt, with some whole Spice:

When you think it is almost enough, put in one pound of Currans well washed and picked, four Ounces of Dates stoned and diced thin, and when they have boiled enough, put in half a pound of sweet Almonds blanched and beaten fine with Rose-water, strain them in with some of the Liquor, then put in some Sack and Sugar; then lay some thin slices of white bread into a deep Dish, and lay your Capon in the midst, then pour your Broth over it.

Garnish your dish with plumped Raisins and Prunes, and serve it in.

70. *To make a Calvesfoot Pie.*

Take six Calves feet tenderly boiled, and cut them in halves, then make some Paste with fine Flower, Butter, cold Cream and the yolk and white of one Egg, rowl it very thin, and lay it into your baking-pan, then lay some butter in the bottom, and then your Calves feet with some large Mace, half a pound of Raisins of the Sun, half a pound of Currans, then lay more butter and close it and bake it, then cut it up, and put in the yolks of three Eggs, some white Wine, Butter and a little Salt, and so serve it to the Table; Garnish your Dish with pretty Conceits made in Paste, and baked a little.

71. *To make an Artichoke Pie.*

Make your Paste as before named, and roul it thin, and lay it into your baking-pan.

Then lay in Butter sliced thin, and then your bottoms of Artichokes tenderly boiled, season it with a little Salt, a little gross Pepper, and some sliced Nutmeg, with a blade or two of Mace and a little Sugar, then lay in some Marrow, Candied Orange and Citron Pill, with some Candied Eringo Roots; then cover it with butter, and close it with your Paste, and so bake it, then cut it up, and put in white Wine, Butter, and the yolks of Eggs and Sugar; cover it again, and serve it to the Table.

72. *To make an Oyster-Pie.*

Make your Paste as before, and lay it in your Pan, then lay in Butter, and then put in as many great Oysters as will almost fill your Pan, with their Liquor strained, some whole Pepper, Mace and Nutmeg; then lay in Marrow and the Yolks of hard Eggs, so cover them with Butter, close them, and bake your Pie, then put in White Wine, Anchovies, Butter and the Yolks of Eggs; cover it again and serve it the Table.

73. *To make a Pig-Pie.*

Take a large Pig and slit it in two, and bone it, onely the two sides, not the head, then having your Paste ready laid in your Pan, and some Butter in the bottom, lay in your Pig, season it with Pepper, Salt, Nutmeg and Mace, and one handful of Sage shred small and mixed with the Spice and Salt, then lay in more Butter, close it, and bake it.

Serve it in cold with Mustard, and garnish your Dish with Bay Leaves.

If you would eat it hot, you must leave out the Pepper and some of the Salt, and put in store of Currans, and when it comes out of the Oven, put in some Butter, Vinegar, and Sugar, and so serve it.

74. *To make a Rasberry Tart.*

Take some Puff-paste rolled thin, and lay it into your Baking-Pan, then lay in your Rasberries and cover them with fine Sugar, then close your Tart and bake it; then cut it up, and put in half a Pint of Cream, the yolks of two or three Eggs well beaten, and a little Sugar; then serve it in cold with the Lid off, and sugar strewed upon the brims of the Dish.

75. *To make a Carp Pie.*

Have your Paste ready laid in your bake-pan, and some Butter in the bottom.

Then take a large Carp, scale him, gut him, and wash him clean, and dry him in a Cloth, then lay him into your Pan with some whole Cloves, Mace, and sliced Nutmeg, with two handfuls of Capers, then put in some White Wine, and mix some Butter with Salt, and lay all over; then close it, and bake it; this is very good to be eaten either hot or cold.

76. *To boil a Goose or Rabbits with Sausages.*

Take a large Goose a little powdered, and boil it very well, or a couple of Rabbits trussed finely; when either of these are almost boiled, put in a Pound of Sausages, and boil them with them, then lay either of these into a Dish, and the Sausages here and there one, with some thin Collops of Bacon fryed, then make for Sauce, Mustard and Butter, and so serve it in.

77. *To make a Fricasie of Veal, Chicken, or Rabbits, or of any thing else.*

Take either of these and cut them into small pieces, then put them into a frying pan with so much water as will cover them with a little salt, whole Spice, Limon Pill and a bundle of sweet herbs, let them boil together till the Meat be tender, then put in some Oysters, and when they are plumped, take a little Wine, either White or Claret, and two Anchovies dissolved therein with some Butter, and put all these to the rest, and when you think your Meat is enough, take it out with a little Skimmer, and put it into a Dish upon Sippets; then put into your Liquor the yolks of Eggs well beaten, and mix them over the fire, then pour it all over your Meat; Garnish your Dish with Barberries, and serve it in; this Dish you may make of raw meat or of cold meat which hath been left at Meals.

78. *To make Scotch Collops of Veal or Mutton.*

Take your meat and slice it very thin, and beat it with a rolling-pin, then hack it all over, and on both sides with the back of a Knife, then fry it with a little Gravie of any Meat, then lay your Scotch Collops into a Dish over a Chafingdish of Coals, and dissolve two Anchovies in Claret Wine, and add to it some butter and the yolks of three Eggs well beaten, heat them together, and pour it over them:

Then lay in some thin Collops of Bacon fryed, some Sausage meat fried, and the yolks of hard Eggs fryed after they are boiled, because they shall look round and brown, so serve it to the Table.

79. *To make a Pudding of a Manchet.*

Take a Manchet, put it into a Posnet, and fill the Posnet up with Cream, then put in Sugar and whole Spice, and let it boil leisurely till all the Cream be wasted away, then put it into a Dish, and take some Rosewater, and Butter and Sugar, and pour over it, so serve it in with fine Sugar strewed all over it.

Your Manchet must be chipped before you put it into the Cream.

80. *To make a Calves head Pie.*

Make your Paste, and lay it into your Pan as before, then lay in Butter, and then your Calves Head, being tenderly boiled, and cut in little thin bits, and seasoned with Pepper, Salt and Nutmeg, then put in some Oysters, Anchovies and Claret Wine, with some yolks of hard Eggs and Marrow, then cover it with Butter, and close it and bake it; when it is baked, eat it hot.

81. *To dry Tongues.*

Take some Pump water and Bay salt, or rather refined Saltpeter, which is better; make a strong Brine therewith, and when the Salt is well melted in it, put in your Tongues, and let them lie one Week, then put them into a new Brine, made in the same manner, and in that let them lie a week longer, then take them out, and dry-salt them with Bay Salt beaten small, till they are as hard as may be, then hang them in the Chimney where you burn Wood, till they are very dry, and you may keep them as long as you please; when you would eat of them, boil them with [Transcriber's note: word missing] in the Pot as well as Water, for that will make them look black, and eat tender, and look red within; when they are cold, serve them in with Mustard and Sugar.

82. *To make Angelot Cheese.*

Take some new Milk and strokings together, the quantity of a Pail full, put some Runnet into it, and stir it well about, and cover it till your Cheese be come, then have ready narrow deep Moats open at both ends, and with your flitting Dish fill your Moats as they stand upon a board, without breaking or wheying the Cheese, and as they sink, still fill them up, and when you see you can turn them, which will be about the next day, keep them with due turning twice in a day, and dry them carefully, and when they are half a year old, they will be fit to be eat.

83. *To make a Hare-Pie.*

Take the flesh of a very large Hare, and beat it in a Mortar with as much Marrow or Beef Suet as the Hare contains, then put in Pepper, Salt, Nutmeg, Cloves and Mace, as much as you judge to be fit, and beat it again till you find they be well mixed, then having your Paste ready in your

Baking-Pan, lay in some Butter, and then your Meat, and then Butter again; so close it, and bake it, and when it is cold, serve it in with Mustard and Sugar, and garnish your Dish with Bay leaves; this will keep much longer than any other Pie.

84. *To rost a Shoulder of Venison or of Mutton in Bloud.*

Take the Bloud of either the Deer or the Sheep, and strain it, and put therein some grated Bread and Salt, and some Thyme plucked from the Stalks, then wrap your Meat in it and rost it, and when you see the bloud to be dry upon it, baste it well with butter, and make sauce for it with Claret Wine, Crums of Bread and Sugar, with some beaten Cinamon, salt it a little in the rosting, but not too much; you may stick it with Rosemary if you will.

85. *To stew a Pig.*

Lay a large Pig to the Fire, and when it is hot, skin it, and cut it into divers pieces, then take some white wine and strong broth, and stew it therein with an Onion or two cut very small, a little Pepper, Salt, Nutmeg, Thyme, and Anchovies, with some Elder Vinegar, sweet Butter and Gravie; when it is enough, lay Sippets of French Bread in your Dish, and put your Meat thereon.

Garnish your Dish with Oranges and Limons.

86. *To make a Fricasie of Sheeps feet.*

Take your Sheeps feet tenderly boiled, and slit them, and take out the knot of hair within, then put them into a Frying-pan with as much water as will cover them, a little Salt, Nutmeg, a blade of Mace, and a bundle of sweet herbs, and some plumped Currans; when they are enough, put in some Butter, and shake them well together, then lay Sippets into a Dish, and put them upon them with a Skimmer, then put into your Liquor a little Vinegar, the yolks of two or three Eggs, and heat it over the fire, and pour it over them; Garnish your Dish with Barberries, and serve it to the Table.

87. *To make a Steak-Pie with Puddings in it.*

Lay your Paste ready in your Pan, and lay some butter in the bottom, then lay a Neck of Mutton cut into steaks thereon, then take some of the best of a Leg of Mutton minced small, with as much Beef Suet as Mutton; season it with beaten Spice and Salt, and a little Wine, Apples shred small, a little Limon Pill, a little Verjuice and Sugar, then put in some Currans, and when they are well mixed, make it into Balls with the yolks of Eggs, and lay them upon the steaks, then put in some Butter and close your Pie and bake it, and serve it in hot.

88. *To dress Salmon or other Fish by Infusion, a very good way.*

Take a Joul of Salmon, or a Tail, or any other part, or any other Fish which you like, put it into a Pot or Pan, with some Vinegar, Water and Salt, Spice, sweet herbs, and white Wine; when it is enough, lay it into a Dish, and take some of the Liquor with an Anchovie or two, a little Butter and the yolks of Eggs beaten; heat these over the fire, and poure over your Fish; if you please, you may put in shrimps, but then you must put in the more Butter; Garnish your Dish with some Limon or Orange, and some Shrimps.

89. *To make Loaves to Butter.*

Take the yolks of twelve Eggs, and six Whites, a little Yeast, Salt and beaten Ginger, wet some Flower with this, and make it into a Paste, let it lie to rise a while, and then make it into Loaves, and prick them, and bake them, then put in white wine and butter and sugar, and serve it in.

90. *To make a Calves Chaldron Pie, and Puddings also of it.*

Take a fat Calves Chaldron boiled tender, and shred it very small, then season it with beaten spice and salt:

Then put in a pound of Currans and somewhat more, and as much Sugar as you think fit, and a little Rosewater; then having your Pie ready, fill it with this, and press it down; close it and bake it, then put some Wine into it, and so eat it.

If you will make Puddings of it, you must add a little Cream and grated bread, a little Sack, more Sugar, and the yolks of Eggs, and so you may bake them, or boil, or fry them.

91. *To make Rice-Cream.*

Boil a quart of Cream, then put in two handfuls of Rice Flower, and a little fine Flower, as much Sugar as is fit, the yolk of an Egg, and some Rosewater.

92. *To make a Pompion-Pie.*

Having your Paste ready in your Pan, put in your Pompion pared and cut in thin slices, then fill up your Pie with sharp Apples, and a little Pepper, and a little Salt, then close it, and bake it, then butter it, and serve it in hot to the Table.

93. *To fry Pompion.*

Cut it in thin slices when it is pared, and steep it in Sack a while, then dip it in Eggs, and fry it in Butter, and put some Sack and Butter for Sauce, so serve it in with salt about the Dish brims.

94. *To make Misers for Children to eat in Afternoons in Summer.*

Take half a Pint of good small Beer, two spoonfuls of Sack, the Crum of half a penny Manchet, two handfuls of Currans washed clean and dried, and a little of grated Nutmeg, and a little Sugar, so give it to them cold.

95. *To fry Toasts.*

Take a twopenny white Loaf, and pare away the Crust, and cut thin slices of it, then dip them first in Cream, then in the yolks of Eggs well beaten, and mixed with beaten Cinamon, then fry them in Butter, and serve them in with Verjuice, Butter and Sugar.

96. *To boil or rather stew Carps in their own Blood.*

Take two fair Carps, and scowr them very well from slime with water and a little salt, then lay them in a Dish and open their bellies, take away their Guts, and save the Blood and Rows in the Dish, then put in a Pint of Claret Wine, some whole Spice and some Salt, with a little Horse-Radish Root, then cover them close, and let them stew over a Chafingdish of Coals, and when they are enough, lay them into a Dish which must be rubbed with a Shelots, and Sippets laid in, then take a little of the Liquor, and an Anchovie or two, with a little Butter, heat them together, and pour it over them, then garnish your Dish with Capers, Oranges or Limons, and serve it in very hot.

97. *To make Fritters.*

Take half a Pint of Sack and a Pint of Ale, a little Yest, the yolks of twelve Eggs, and six Whites, with some beaten Spice and a very little salt, make this into thick Batter with fine Flower, then boil your Lard, and dip round thin slices of Apples in this Batter, and fry them; serve them in with beaten spice and sugar.

98. *To pickle Coleflowers.*

Take some white wine Vinegar and salt, with some whole Spice, boil them together very well, then put in your Coleflowers, and cover them, and let them stand upon Embers for one hour, then take them out, and when they are cold, put them into a Pot, and boil the Liquor again with more Vinegar, and when it is cold, put it to them, and keep them close from the Air.

99. *To preserve Orange or Limon Pills in thin slices in Jelly.*

Take the most beautiful and thickest Rinds, and then cut them in halves, and take their Meat clean out, then boil them in several waters till a straw will run through them, then wash them in cold water, and pick them and dry them:

Then take to a Pound of these, one quart of water wherein thin slices of Pippins have been boiled, and that the water feels slippery, take to this water three pounds of Sugar, and make thereof a Syrup, then put in your

Pills and scald them, and set them by till the next day, then boil them till you find that the Syrup will jelly, then lay your Pills into your Glasses, and put into your Syrup the Juice of three Oranges and one Limon; then boil it again till it be a stiff Jelly, and put it to them.

100. *To make Cakes of the Pulp of Limons, or rather the Juice of Limons.*

Take out all the juice part of the Limon without breaking the little skins which hold it, then boil some Sugar to a Candy height, and put in this Juice, and stir it about, and immediately put it into a warm Stove, and put in fire twice or thrice a day; when you see that it doth Candy on the one side, then turn them out of the Glasses with a wet knife on the other upon a sleeked Paper, and then let that candy also, and put them up in a Box with Papers between them.

101. *To make good minced Pies.*

Take one pound and half of Veal parboiled, and as much Suet, shred them very fine, then put in 2 pound of Raisins, 2 pound of Currans, 1 pound of Prunes, 6 Dates, some beaten Spice, a few Caraway seeds, a little Salt, Verjuice, Rosewater and Sugar, to fill your Pies, and let them stand one hour in the Oven:

When they go to Table strew on fine Sugar.

102. *To make a Loaf of Curds.*

Take the Curds of three quarts of Milk rubbed together with a little Flower, then put in a little beaten Ginger, and a little Salt, half a Pint of Yest, the yolks of ten Eggs, and three Whites: work these into a stiff Paste with so much Flower as you see fit, then lay it to rise in a warm Cloth a while, then put in Butter, Sugar, Sack, and some beaten Spice, and so serve it in.

103. *To make Cheese Loaves.*

Take the Curds of three quarts of Milk, and as much grated Bread as Curd, the yolks of twelve Eggs, and six Whites, some Cream, a little Flower, and beaten Spice, a little Salt, and a little Sack; when you have made it in a stiff Paste with a little flower, roul some of it thin to fry, and serve them in with beaten Spice and Sugar strewed over them.

Then make the rest into a Loaf, and bake it, then cut it open, and serve it in with Cream, Butter and Sugar.

104. *To fry Oysters.*

Take of your largest Oysters, wash them and dry them, and beat an Egg or two very well, and dip them in that, and so fry them, then take their Liquor, and put an Anchovy to it, and some Butter, and heat them together over the fire, and having put your fryed Oysters in a Dish, pour the Sawce over them and serve them in.

105. *To broil Oysters.*

Take your largest Oysters, and put them into Scollop Shells, or into the biggest Oyster shells with their own Liquor, and set them upon a Gridiron over Charcoals, and when you see they be boiled in the Liquor, put in some Butter, a few Crums of Bread, and a little Salt, then let them stand till they are very brown, and serve them to the Table in the Shells upon a Dish and Pie-Plate.

106. *To rost Oysters.*

Take the largest, and spit them upon little long sticks, and tie them to the Spit, then lay them down to the fire, and when they are dry, bast them with Claret Wine, and put into your Pan two Anchovies, and two or three Bay-leaves, when you think they are enough, bast them with Butter, and dredge them, and take a little of that liquor in the Pan, and some Butter, and heat it in a Porringer, and pour over them.

107. *To make most excellent and delicate Pies.*

Take two Neats tongues tenderly boiled, and peel them, and mince them small with some Beef Suet or Marrow, then take a pound of Currans and a pound of Raisins of the Sun stoned, some beaten Spice, Rosewater, a little Salt, a little Sack and Sugar.

Beat all these with the minced meat in a Mortar till it come to a perfect Paste, then having your Paste ready laid in your baking-Pan, fill it or them with this meat, then lay on the top some sliced Dates, and so close them, and bake them, when they are cold they will cut smooth like Marmalade.

108. *To make fine Custards.*

Take two quarts of Cream and boil it well with whole Spice, then put in the yolks of twelve Eggs, and six Whites well beaten and strained, then put in these Eggs over the fire, and keep them stirring lest they turn, then when they are thoroughly hot, take it off and stir it till it be almost cold, then put in Rosewater and Sugar, and take out the whole Spice, then put your Custard into several things to bake, and do not let them stand too long in the Oven; when you serve them in, strew on small French Comfits of divers colours, or else fine Sugar, which you please.

109. *To make a Stump Pie.*

Take a pound of Veal and as much Suet, parboil your Veal, and shred them together, but not very small, then put in one pound of Raisins, one pound of Currans, four Ounces of Dates stoned and sliced thin, some beaten Spice, Rosewater and Sugar, and a little Salt, then take the yolks of Eggs well beaten, and mix amongst the rest of the things very well, then having your Pie ready, fill it and press it down, then lid it, and bake it.

110. *To make Egg-Pies.*

Take the yolks of eight hard Eggs, and shred them small with their weight of Beef Suet minced very small also, then put in one pound of Currans, four Ounces of Dates stoned and sliced, some beaten Spice, Limon pill, Rosewater and Sugar, and a little Salt, mix them well together, if you please, you may put in an Apple shred small, so fill your Pies and bake them, but not too much, serve them to the Table with a little Wine.

111. *To make hashed Meat.*

Take a Leg or Shoulder of Mutton, lay it down to the fire, and as it doth rost, cut it off in little bits, and let it lie in the Pan, bast it with Claret wine and Butter, and a little Salt, and put two or three Shelots in your Pan, when you have cut off so much as you can, lay the bones into a Dish over a Chafingdish of Coals, and put your Meat to it with the Liquor, and two

Anchovies, cover it, and let it stew a while; when it is enough, put in some Capers, and serve it in with Sippets; Garnish your Dish with Olives and Capers, and Samphire; thus you may do with any cold meat between two Dishes.

112. *To make a Fricasie of Oysters.*

Take a quart of Oysters and put them into a frying pan with some white Wine and their own Liquor, a little Salt, and some whole Spice, and two or three Bay Leaves, when you think they be enough, lay them in a dish well warmed, then add to their Liquor two Anchovies, some Butter, and the yolks of four Eggs; Garnish your Dish with Barberries.

113. *To make a Fricasie of Eels.*

Take a midling sort of Eels, scour them well, and cut off the heads and throw them away, then gut them, and cut them in pieces, then put them into a frying pan with so much white Wine and water as will cover them, then put in whole Spice, a bundle of sweet herbs and a little Salt, let them boil, and when they be very tender, take them up and lay them into a warm Dish, then add to their Liquor two Anchovies, some Butter and the yolks of Eggs, and pour over them:

Thus you may make Fricasies of Cockles or of Shrimps, or Prawns.

Garnish your Dish with Limon and Barberries.

114. *To make an Eel-Pie.*

Take your largest Eels, and flay them, and cut them in pieces, then having your Pie ready with Butter in the bottom, season your Eels with Pepper, Salt and Nutmeg, then lay them in and cover them with Butter, so close it and bake it, if you please, you may put in some Raisins of the Sun, and some large Mace, it is good hot or cold.

115. *To souce an Eel and Collar it.*

Take a very large fat Eel and scour it well, throw away the head and gut her, and slit her down the back, season her with Pepper, Salt, Nutmeg and Mace, then boil her in white Wine, and Salt and Water, with a bundle of sweet herbs and some Limon Pill, when it is well boiled, take it up and lay it to cool; then put good store of Vinegar into the Liquor, and when it is cold, put in your Eel, and keep it:

You must roul it up in a Collar and tie it hard with a Tape, and sew it up in a Cloth, then put it in to boil; when it hath lain a week, serve it to the Table with a Rosemary Branch in the middle, and Bay Leaves round the Dish sides, eat it with Mustard.

116. *To stew Eels.*

Take them without their heads, flay them and cut them in pieces, then fill a Posnet with them, and set them all on end one by one close to one another, and put in so much White Wine and Water as will cover them, then put in good store of Currans to them, whole Spice, sweet herbs, and a little Salt, cover them and let them stew, and when they are very tender, put in some Butter, and so shake them well, and serve them upon Sippets; Garnish your Dish with Orange or Limon and raw Parsley.

117. *To make a Herring Pie.*

Take four of the best pickled Herrings, and skin them, then split them and bone them, then having your Pie in readiness with Butter in the bottom, then lay your Herrings in halves into your Pie one lay of them, then put in Raisins, Currans and Nutmeg, and a little Sugar, then lay in more Butter, then more Herrings, Fruit and Spice, and more Butter, and so close it, and bake it; your Herrings must be well watered.

118. *To rost a Pike and to lard it.*

Take a large Pike, and scale it, gut it, and wash it clean, then lard it on the back with pickled Herring and Limon Pill, then spit it and lay it down to the fire to rost, bast it often with Claret Wine and Butter, when it is enough, make Sauce for it with Claret Wine and Butter, and serve it in.

119. *To boil fresh Salmon.*

Take a Joll or a Tail of fresh Salmon, then take Vinegar and Water, Salt and whole Spice, and boil them together, then put in your Salmon, and when it is boiled, take some Butter and some of the Liquor with an Anchovie or two, and a little white Wine and a quart of Shrimps out of their Shells, heat these together, and so Dish your Salmon, and pour this over it.

Garnish your Dish with Shrimps and Anchovies, and Slices of Limon.

120. *To boil a Cods Head.*

Boil Wine, Water and Salt together, with whole Spice and sweet herbs, and a little Horse-Radish Root, then put in your Cods head, and boil it very well, then drain it well from the Water, and lay it in a dish over a Chafingdish of Coals:

Then take some of the Liquor and two Anchovies, some butter and some Shrimps, heat them over the fire, and pour over it, then poach some Eggs and lay over it, and also about the Brims of the Dish; Garnish your Dish with Limon and Barberries, so serve it to the Table very hot:

Thus you may do Haddocks or Whitings, or any other fresh Fish you like best.

121. *To make Olives of Veal.*

Take thin slices of a Leg of Veal, and have ready some Suet finely shred, some Currans, beaten Spice, sweet herbs, and hard yolks of Eggs, and a little salt mixed well together, then strew it upon the insides of your slices of Meat, and roul them up hard, and make them fast with a scure, so spit them and roste them, baste them with Butter, and serve them in with Vinegar, Butter and Sugar.

122. *To make an Olive Pie.*

Having your Paste in readiness with Butter in the bottom, lay in some of the forenamed Olives, but not fastned with a Scure, then put in Currans, hard Eggs, and sweet Butter, with some herbs shred fine; be sure you cover it well with Butter, and put in a little white Wine and Sugar, and close it, and bake it, eat it hot or cold, but hot is better.

123. *To make a Ball to take Stains out of Linnen, which many times happens by Cooking or Preserving.*

Take four Ounces of hard white Sope, beat it in a Mortar, with two small Limons sliced, and as much Roch Allom as a Hazle Nut, when they are beaten well together, make it up in little Balls, rub the stain therewith and then wash it in warm water, till you see it be quite out.

124. *To make a fine Pomander.*

Take two Ounces of Laudanum, of Benjamin and Storax one Ounce, Musk six gr. as much of Civet, as much of Ambergreece, of Calamus Aromaticus, and Lignum Aloes, of each the weight of a Groat, beat all these in a hot Mortar and with a hot Pestel, till it come to a perfect Paste, then take a little Gum Dragon steeped in Rosewater, and rub your hand withal, and make it up with speed, and dry them, but first make them into what shapes you please, and print them.

125. *A very fine washing-Ball.*

Take three Ounces of Orrice, half an Ounce of Cypress-wood, 2 Ounces of Calamus Aromaticus, 1 ounce of Damask-Rose leaves, 2 Ounces of Lavender-flowers, a quarter of an Ounce of Cloves, beat all these and searce them fine, then take two pounds and an half of Castile Sope dissolved in Rose water, and beat all these forenamed things with the Sope in a Mortar, and when they are well incorporated, make it into Balls, and keep them in a Box with Cotton as long as you please.

126. *To make French Broth called Kink.*

Take a leg of Beef and set it over the fire with a good quantity of fair water, when it boils, scum it, and what meat soever you have to dress that day, either of Fowl or small meat, put it all into this Liquor and parboil it, then take out those small meats, and put in some French Barley, and some whole Spice, one Clove or two of Garlick, and a handful of Leeks, and some Salt; when it is boiled enough, pour it from the Barley, and in put a little Saffron; so serve it in; and garnish your Dish with sliced Oranges or Limons, and put a little of the juice therein.

127. *To make Broth of a Lambs Head.*

Boil it with as much water as will cover it, with whole Spice, and a little Salt, and a bundle of sweet herbs, then put in strained Oatmeal and Cream, and some Currans, when you take it up, put in Sack and Sugar, then lay the Head in a Dish, and put the Broth to it, and serve it in.

128. *To season a Chicken-Pie.*

Having your Paste rolled thin, and laid into your baking-pan, lay in some Butter, then lay in your Chickens quartered, and seasoned with Pepper, Nutmeg and a little Salt, then put in Raisins, Currans, and Dates, then lay Butter on the top, close it and bake it, then cut it up, and put in Clouted Cream, Sack and Sugar.

129. *To make an Herb Pie.*

Take Spinage, hard Lettice, and a few sweet herbs, pick them, wash them, and shred them, and put them into your Pie with Butter, and Nutmeg and Sugar, and a little Salt, to close it and bake it, then draw it and open it, and put in Clouted Cream; Sack and Sugar, and stir it well together, and serve it in.

130. *To roste Lobsters.*

Take two fair Lobsters alive, wash them clean, and stop the holes as you do to boil, then fasten them to a Spit, the insides together; make a good fire, and strew Salt on them, and that will kill them quickly, bast them with Water and Salt till they be very red, then have ready some Oysters stewed and cut small; put them into a Dish with melted Butter beaten thick with a little water, then take a few spoonfuls of the Liquor of the stewed Oysters, and dissolve in it two Anchovies, then put it to the melted Butter, then take up your Lobsters, and crack the shells that they may be easie to open.

131. *To make a Pumpion Pie.*

Take a Pumpion, pare it, and cut it in thin slices, dip it in beaten Eggs and Herbs shred small, and fry it till it be enough, then lay it into a Pie with Butter, Raisins, Currans, Sugar and Sack, and in the bottom some sharp Apples; when it is baked, butter it and serve it in.

132. *To make an Artichoke Pudding.*

Boil a quart of Cream with whole Spice, then put in half a pound of sweet Almonds blanched, and beaten with Rosewater; when they have boiled well, take it from the fire, and take out the Spice, when it is almost cold, put in the yolks of ten Eggs, some Marrow and some bottoms of Artichokes, then sweeten it with Sugar and put in a little Salt, then butter a Dish, and bake it in it, serve it to the Table stuck full of blanched Almonds, and fine Sugar strewed over it.

133. *To pickle Sprats like Anchovies.*

Take a Peck of the biggest Sprats without their heads, and salt them a little over night, then take a Pot or Barrel, and lay in it a Lay of Bay salt, and then a lay of Sprats, and a few Bay leaves, then salt again; thus do till you have filled the Vessel, put in a little Limon Pill also among your Bay leaves, then cover the Vessel and pitch it, that no Air get in, set it in a cool Cellar, and once in a week turn it upside down; in three Months you may eat of them.

134. *To keep Artichokes all the Year.*

Gather your Artichokes with long stalks, and then cut off the stalks close to them, then boil some water, with good Pears and Apples sliced thin, and the Pith of the great stalks, and a Quince or two quartered to give it a relish; when these have boiled a while, put in your Artichokes, and boil all together till they be tender, then take them up and set them to cool, then boil your Liquor well and strain it, when your Artichokes be cold, put them into your Barrel, and when the Liquor is cold, pour it over them, so cover it close that no Air get in.

135. *To make Pasty of a Joll of Ling.*

Make your Crust with fine Flower, Butter, cold Cream, and two yolks of Eggs:

Roul it thin and lay it in your Bake-pan, then take part of a Joll of Ling well boiled, and pull it all in Bits, then lay some Butter into your Pasty and then the Ling, then some grated Nutmeg, sliced Ginger, Cloves and Mace, Oysters, Muscles, Cockles, and Shrimps, the yolks of raw Eggs, a few Comfits perfumed, Candied Orange Pill, Citron Pill, and Limon Pill, with Eringo Roots:

Then put in white Wine, and good store of Butter, and put on a thick lid, when it is baked, open it, and let out the steam.

136. *To make French Servels.*

Take cold Gammon of Bacon, fat and lean together, cut it small as for Sausages, season it with Pepper, Cloves and Mace, and a little Shelots, knead it into a Paste with the yolks of Eggs, and fill some Bullocks Guts with it, and boil them; but if you would have them to keep, then do not put in Eggs.

When you have filled the Guts, boil them, and hang them up, and when you would eat them, serve them in thin slices with a Sallad.

137. *To make a Pallat Pie.*

Take Oxe Pallats and boil them so tender that you may run a straw through them; to three Palates take six Sheeps tongues boiled tender and peeled, three sweet-Breads of Veal, cut all these in thin slices, then having your Pie ready, and Butter in the bottom, lay in these things, first seasoned with Pepper, Salt and Nutmeg, and Thyme and Parsley shred small, and as the Season of the year is, put into it Asparagus, Anchovies, Chesnuts, or what you please else, as Candied Orange Pill, Limon Pill, or Citron Pill, with Eringo roots, and yolks of hard Eggs, some Marrow and some Oysters, then lay in good store of Butter on the top, so close it and bake it, then put in white Wine, buter, the yolks of Eggs, and Vinegar and Sugar; heat them together over the fire, and serve it in.

138. *To make Sauce for Fowles or Mutton.*

Take Claret Wine, Vinegar, Anchovies, Oisters, Nutmeg, Shelot, Gravie of Mutton or Beef, sweet Butter, Juice of Limon, and a little Salt, and if you please Orange or Limon Pill.

139. *To make Oat-Cakes.*

Take fine Flower, and mix it very well with new Ale Yest, and make it very stiff, then make it into little Cakes, and roul them very thin, then lay them on an Iron to bake, or on a baking stone, and make but a slow fire under it, and as they are baking, take them and turn the edges of them round on the Iron, that they may bake also, one quarter of an hour will bake them; a little before you take them up, turn them on the other side, only to flat them; for if you turn them too soon, it will hinder the rising, the Iron or Stone whereon they are baked, must stand at a distance from the fire.

140. *To make a rare Lamb Pie.*

Take a Leg of Lamb, and take the meat clean out of it at the great end, but keep the skin whole, then press the Meat in a Cloth, and mince it small, and put as much Beef Suet to it as the Meat in weight, and mince it small, then put to it Naples Bisket grated fine, season it with beaten Spice, Rosewater, and a little Salt, then put in some Candied Limon Pill, Orange Pill, and Citron Pill shred small, and some Sugar, then put part of the Meat into the skin, then having your Pie in readiness, and Butter in the bottom, lay in this Meat, then take the rest of your Meat, and make it into Balls or Puddings with yolks of Eggs, then lay them into the Pie to fill up the Corners, then take Candied Orange, Limon and Citron Pill, cut in long narrow slices and strew over it; you may put in Currans and Dates if you please, then lay on Butter, and close up your Pie and bake it, and leave a Tunnel, when it is baked, put in Sack, Sugar, yolks of Eggs and Butter heat together, if you put in Marrow, it will be the better.

141. *To fry Garden Beans.*

Boil them and blanch them, and fry them in Sweet Butter, with Parsley and shred Onions and a little Salt, then melt Butter for the Sauce.

142. *To make a Sorrel Sallad.*

Take a quantity of French Sorrel picked clean and washed, boil it with water and a little Salt, and when it is enough, drain it and butter it, and put in a little Vinegar and Sugar into it, then garnish it with hard Eggs and Raisins.

143. *To make good cold Sallads of several things.*

Take either Coleflowers, or Carrots, or Parsneps, or Turneps after they are well boiled, and serve them in with Oil, Vinegar and Pepper, also the Roots of red Beets boiled tender are very good in the same manner.

144. *To make the best sort of Pippin Paste.*

Take a pound of raw Pippins sliced and beaten in a Mortar, then take a pound of fine Sugar and boil it to a candy height with a little fair water, then put in your Pippins, and boil it till it will come from the bottom of the Posnet, but stir it for fear it burn.

145. *To make Sauce for a Leg of Veal rosted.*

Take boiled Currans, and boiled Parsley, and hard Eggs and Butter and Sugar hot together.

146. *To make Sauce for a Leg of Mutton rosted with Chesnuts.*

Take a good quantity of Chesnuts, and boil them tender, then take the shells off, and bruise them small, then put to them Claret Wine, Butter and a little Salt, so put it into the Dish to the Meat, and serve it in.

147. *To keep Quinces white, either to preserve whole, or for white Marmalade or Paste.*

Coddle them with white Wine and Water, and cover them with sliced Pippins in the Codling.

148. *To make little Pasties with sweet Meats to fry.*

Make some Paste with cold water, butter and flower, with the yolk of an Egg, then roul it out in little thin Cakes, and lay one spoonful of any kind of Sweet meats you like best upon every one, so close them up and fry them with Butter, and serve them in with fine Sugar strewed on.

149. *To boil a Capon on the French fashion.*

Boil your Capon in water and salt, and a little dusty Oatmeal to make it look white, then take two or three Ladles full of Mutton Broth, a Faggot of sweet herbs, two or three Dates cut in long pieces, a few parboiled Currans, and a little whole Pepper, a little Mace and Nutmeg, thicken it with Almonds; season it with Verjuice, Sugar, and a little sweet Butter, then take up your Capon and lard it well with preserved Limon, then lay it in a deep Dish, and pour the broth upon it; then Garnish your Dish with Suckets and preserved Barberries.

150. *To Souce a Pike, Carp or Bream.*

Draw your Fish, but scale it not, and save the Liver of it; wash it very well, then take white Wine, as much water again as Wine, boil them together with whole Spice, Salt and a bundle of sweet Herbs, and when boiles put in your Fish, and just before it a little Vinegar; for that will make it crisp: when it is enough, take it up and put it into a Trey, then put into the Liquor some whole Pepper, and whole Ginger, and when it is boiled enough, take it off and cool it, and when it is quite cold, put in your Fish, and when you serve it in, lay some of the Jelly about the Dish sides, and some Fennel and Sawcers of Vinegar.

151. *To boil a Gurnet on the French fashion.*

Draw your Gurnet and wash it, boil it in water and salt and a bundle of sweet herbs; when it is enough, take it up and put it into a Dish with Sippets over a Chafingdish of Coals; then take Verjuice, Butter, Nutmeg and Pepper, and the yolks of two Eggs, heat it together, and pour over it; Garnish your Dish as you please.

152. *To rost a Leg of Mutton on the French fashion.*

Take a Leg of Mutton, and pare off all the Skin as thin as you can, then lard it with sweet Lard, and stick it with Cloves, when it is half rosted, cut off three or four thin pieces, and mince it with sweet herbs, and a little beaten Ginger, put in a Ladle full of Claret wine, and a little sweet butter, two sponfuls of Verjuice and a little Pepper, a few Capers, then chop the yolks of two hard Eggs in it, then when these have stewed a while in a Dish, put your bonie part which is rosted into a Dish, and pour this on it and serve it in.

153. *To rost a Neats tongue.*

Chop sweet herbs fine with a piece of raw Apple, season it with Pepper and Ginger, and the yolk of an Egg made hard and minced small, then stuff your Tongue with this, and rost it well, and baste it with Butter and Wine; when it is enough, take Verjuice, Butter, and the Juice of a Limon, and a little Nutmeg, then Dish your Tongue and pour this Sauce over it and serve it in.

154. *To boil Pigeons with Rice.*

Take your Pigeons and truss them, and stuff their bellies with sweet herbs, then put them into a Pipkin with as much Mutton broth as will cover them, with a blade of Mace and some whole Pepper; boil all these together until the Pigeons be tender, and put in Salt:

Then take them from the fire, and scum off the Fat very clean, then put in a piece of sweet Butter, season it with Verjuice, Nutmeg and a little Sugar, thicken it with Rice boiled in sweet Cream. Garnish your Dish with preserved Barberries and Skirret Roots boiled tender.

155. *To boil a Rabbit.*

Take a large Rabbit, truss it and boil it with a little Mutton Broth, white Wine and a blade of Mace, then take Lettuce, Spinage, and Parsley, Winter-Savory and sweet Marjoram, pick all these and wash them clean, and bruise them a little to make the Broth look green, thicken it with the Crust of a Manchet first steeped in a little Broth, and put in a little sweet Butter, season it with Verjuice and Pepper, and serve it to the Table upon Sippets; Garnish the Dish with Barberries.

156. *To boil a Teal or Wigeon.*

Parboil either of these Fowls and throw them into a pail of fair Water, for that taketh away the Rankness, then rost them half, and take them from the fire, and put sweet herbs in the bellies of them, and stick the Brests with Cloaves, then put them in a Pipkin with two or three ladles full of Mutton broth, very strong of the Meat, a blade of whole Mace, two or three little Onions minced small; thicken it with a Toast of Houshold bread, and put in a little Butter, then put in a little Verjuice, so take it up and serve it.

157. *To boil Chickens or Pigeons with Goosberries or Grapes.*

Boil them with Mutton Broth and white Wine, with a blade of Mace and a little Salt, and let their bellies be filled with sweet herbs, when they are tender thicken the Broth with a piece of Manchet, and the yolks of two hard Eggs, strained with some of the Broth, and put it into a deep Dish with some Verjuice and Butter and Sugar, then having Goosberries or Grapes tenderly scalded, put them into it, then lay your Chickens or Pigeons into a Dish, and pour the Sauce over them, and serve them in.

158. *A made Dish of Rabbits Livers.*

Take six Livers and chop them fine with sweet herbs and the yolks of two hard Eggs, season it with beaten Spice, and Salt, and put in some plumped Currans, and a little melted Butter, so mix them very well together, and having some Paste ready rouled thin, make it into little Pasties and fry them, strew Sugar over them and serve them.

159. *To make a Florentine with the Brawn of a Capon, or the Kidney of Veal.*

Mince any of these with sweet Herbs, then put in parboiled Currans, and Dates minced small, and a little Orange or Limon Pill which is Candied shred small, season it with beaten Spice and Sugar, then take the yolks of two hard Eggs and bruise them with a little Cream, a piece of a short Cake grated, and Marrow cut in short pieces, mix all these together with the forenamed Meat, and put in a little Salt and a little Rosewater, and bake it in a Dish in a Puff-Past, and when you serve it strew Sugar over it.

160. *A Friday Pie without Fish or Flesh.*

Wash a good quantity of green Beets, and pluck out the middle string, then chop them small, with two or three ripe Apples well relished, season it with Pepper, Salt, and Ginger, then add to it some Currans, and having your Pie ready, and Butter in the bottom, put in these herbs, and with them a little Sugar, then put Butter on the top, and close and bake it, then cut it up, and put in the juice of a Limon and Sugar.

161. *To make Umble Pies.*

Boil them very tender, and mince them very small with Beef Suet and Marrow then season it with beaten Spice and Salt, Rosewater and Sugar and a little Sack, so put it into your Paste with Currans and Dates.

162. *To bake Chickens with Grapes.*

Scald your Chickens and truss them, and season them with Pepper, Salt and Nutmeg, and having your Pie ready, and Butter laid in the bottom, put in your Chickens, and then more butter, and bake them with a thin Lid on

You may bake it if you please in a baking-pan.

176. *To make a Pudding of Goose Blood.*

Save the blood of a Goose, and strain it, then put in fine Oatmeal steeped in warm Milk, Nutmeg, Pepper, sweet Herbs, Sugar, Salt, Suet minced fine, Rosewater, Limon Pill, Coriander seeds, then put in some Eggs, and beat all these together very well, then boil them how you do like, either in a buttered Cloth or in Skins, or rost it within the Neck of the Goose.

177. *To make Liver Puddings.*

Take a Hogs Liver boiled and cold, grate it like Bread, then take new Milk and the Fat of a Hog minced fine, put it to the Bread and the Liver, and divide it into two parts, then dry herbs or other if you can minced fine, and put the Herbs into one part with beaten Spice, Anniseeds, Rosewater, Cream and Eggs, Sugar and Salt, so fill the Skins and boil them.

To the other part put preserved Barberries, diced Dates, Currans, beaten Spice, Salt, Sugar, Rosewater, Cream and Eggs, so mix them well together, and fill the Skins and boil them.

178. *To make a Chiveridge Pudding.*

Take the fattest Guts of your Hog clean scoured, then fluff them with beaten Spice and sliced Dates, sweet herbs, a little Salt, Rosewater, Sugar, and two or three Eggs to make it slide; so fill them, tie them up like Puddings and boil them; when they are enough serve them.

179. *To make Rice Puddings in Skins.*

Take two quarts of Milk and put therein as it is yet cold, two good handfuls of Rice clean picked and washed, set it over a slow fire and stir it often, but gently; when you perceive it to swell, let it boil apace till it be tender and very thick, then take it from the fire, and when it is cold, put in six Eggs well beaten, some Rosewater and Sugar, beaten Spice and a little Salt, preserved Barberries and Dates minced small, some Marrow and Citron Pill; mingle them well together and fill your Skins, and boil them.

180. *To make a stewed Pudding.*

Take the yolks of three Eggs and one White, six spoonfuls of sweet Cream, a little beaten spice, and a quarter of a pound of Sewet minced fine, a quarter of a pound of Currans, and a little grated bread, Rosewater, Sugar and Salt; mingle them well together, and wrap them up in little pieces of the Cawl of Veal, and fasten them with a little stick, and tie each end with a stick, you may put four in one dish, then take half a pint of strong Mutton Broth, and 6 spoonfuls of Vinegar, three or four blades of large Mace, and one Ounce of Sugar, make this to boil over a Chafingdish of Coals, then put in your Puddings, and when they boil, cover them with another Dish, but turn them sometimes, and when you see that they are enough, take your Puddings and lay them in a warm Dish upon Sippets, then add to their Broth some Sack, Sugar, and Butter, and pour over them; garnish your Dish with Limon and Barberries.

181. *To make a* Sussex *Pudding.*

Take a little cold Cream, Butter and Flower, with some beaten Spice, Eggs, and a little Salt, make them into a stiff Paste, then make it up in a round Ball, and as you mold it, put in a great piece of Butter in the middle; and so tye it hard up in a buttered Cloth, and put it into boiling water, and let it boil apace till it be enough, then serve it in, and garnish your dish with Barberries; when it is at the Table cut it open at the top, and there will be as it were a Pound of Butter, then put Rosewater and Sugar into it, and so eat it.

In some of this like Paste you may wrap great Apples, being pared whole, in one piece of thin Paste, and so close it round the Apple, and throw them into boiling water, and let them boil till they are enough, you may also put some green Goosberries into some, and when either of these are boiled, cut them open and put in Rosewater Butter and Sugar.

182. *To make* French *Puffs*.

Take Spinage Parsley and Endive, with a little Winter savory, and wash them, and mince them very fine; season them with Nutmeg, Ginger and Sugar, season them with Eggs, and put in a little Salt, then cut a Limon into thin round slices, and upon every slice of Limon lay one spoonful of it.

Then fry them, and serve them in upon some Sippets, and pour over them Sack, Sugar and butter.

183. *To make Apple Puffs*.

Take a Pomewater, or any other Apple that is not hard or harsh in taste, mince it with a few Raisins of the Sun stoned, then wet them with Eggs, and beat them together with the back of a Spoon, season them with Nutmeg, Rosewater, Sugar, and Ginger, drop them into a frying pan with a Spoon into hot Butter, and fry them, then serve them in with the juice of an Orange and a little Sugar and Butter.

184. *To make Kickshaws, to bake or fry in what shape you please.*

Take some Puff-paste and roul it thin, if you have Moulds work it upon them with preserved Pippins, and so close them, and fry or bake them, but when you have closed them you must dip them in the yolks of Eggs, and that will keep all in; fill some with Goosberries, Rasberries, Curd, Marrow, Sweet-breads, Lambs Stones, Kidney of Veal, or any other thing what you like best, either of them being seasoned before you put them in according to your mind, and when they are baked or fryed, strew Sugar on them, and serve them in.

185. *To make an* Italian *Pudding.*

Take a penny white loaf and pare off the crust, then cut it like Dice, then take some Beef Suet shred small, and half a pound of Raisins of the Sun stoned, with as many Currans, mingle them together and season them with beaten Spice and a little Salt, wet them with four Eggs, and stir them gently for fear of breaking the Bread, then put it in a dish with a little Cream and Rosewater and Sugar, then put in some Marrow and Dates, and so butter a dish and bake it, then strew on Sugar and serve it.

186. *To hash Calves Tongues.*

Boil them tender and pill them, then lard them with Limon Pill, and lard them also with fat Bacon, then lay them to the Fire and half rost them; then put them in a Pipkin with Claret Wine, whole Spice and sliced Limon, and a few Caraway Seeds, a little Rosemary and a little Salt, boil all together and serve them in upon Toasts. Thus you may do with Sheeps Tongues also.

187. *To boil a Capon.*

Take strong Mutton Broth, and truss a Capon, and boil him in it with some Marrow and a little Salt in a Pipkin, when it is tender, then put in a pint of White Wine, half a pound of Sugar, and four Ounces of Dates stoned and sliced, Potato Roots boiled and blanched, large Mace and Nutmeg sliced, boil all these together with a quarter of a pint of Verjuyce, then dish the Capon, and add to the Broth the yolks of six Eggs beaten with Sack, and so serve it; garnish dish with several sorts of Candied Pills and Preserved Barberries, and sliced Limon with Sugar upon every slice.

188. *To boil a Capon with Rice.*

Truss your Capon and boil him in water and salt, then take a quarter of a pound of Rice, first boiled in Milk, and put in with some whole Spice and a little Salt, when it is almost enough put in a little Rosewater, and half a pound of Almonds blanched and beaten, strain them in, and put in some Cream and Sugar, then when your Capon is enough, lay it in a dish, and pour the Broth thereon; garnish your Dish as you please, and serve it in.

189. *To boil a Capon with Pippins.*

Parboil your capon after it is trussed, then put it into a pipkin with Mutton Broth and Marrow, and a little Salt, with a quart of White-Wine, a little Nutmeg and Dates stoned and sliced, then put in a quarter of a pound of fine Sugar, then take some Pippins stewed with Sugar, Spice and a little water, and put them in, then lay your Capon into a Dish, and lay some Naples Biskets for Sippets, then bruise the yolks of eight hard Eggs and put into your Broth, with a little Sack, and pour it over your Capon; Garnish your Dish and serve it in.

190. *To boil Chickens with Lettuce the very best way.*

Parboil your Chickens and cut them in Quarters, and put them into a Pipkin with some Mutton Broth, and two or three sweet Breads of Veal, and some Marrow, and some Cloves, and a little Salt, and a little Limon Pill; then take good store of hard Lettuce, cut them in halves and wash them, and put them in; then put in Butter and Sack and white Wine, with a little Mace and Nutmeg, and sliced Dates, let all these stew upon the Fire, and when they be enough, serve them in with Toasts of white Bread for Sippets; Garnish the Dish with Limon and Barberies, and what else you please; thus you may do Pigeons.

190. [Transcriber's Note: so numbered in original] *To boil a Rabbit with Grapes or with Goosberries.*

Truss your Rabbit whole, and boil it in some Mutton Broth till it be tender;

Then take a pint of White Wine, and a good handful of Spinage chopped, the yolks of hard Eggs cut in quarters, put these to the Rabbit with some large Mace; a Fagot of sweet Herbs and a little Salt and some Butter, let them boil together a while, then take your Rabbet and lay it in a Dish and some Sippets, then lay over it some Grapes or Goosberries, scalded with Sugar, and pour your Broth over it.

191. *To boil a Rabbit with Claret Wine.*

Boil a Rabbet as before, then slice Onions and a Carrot root, a few Currans and a Fagot of sweet herbs, and a little Salt, minced Parsley, Barberries picked, large Mace, Nutmeg and Ginger, put all these into a Pipkin with the Rabbet, half a Pound of Butter, and a Pint of Claret

Wine, and let them boil together till it be enough, then serve it upon Sippets.

192. *To boil a wild Duck.*

Truss and parboil it, then half rost it, then carve it, and save the Gravie, then take Onions and Parsley sliced, Ginger and Pepper, put the Gravie into a Pipkin, with Currans, Mace, Barberries, and a quart of Claret Wine, and a little Salt, put your Duck with all the forenamed things into it, and let them boil till it be enough, then put in butter and sugar, and serve it in upon Sippets.

193. *To boil a tame Duck.*

Take your Duck and truss it, and boil it with water and salt, or rather Mutton broth, when it hath boiled a while, put in some whole Spice, and when it is boiled enough, take some white wine and butter, and good store of Onions boiled tender in several waters, with a little of the Liquor wherein the Duck hath boiled, and a little Salt: put your Duck into a Dish, and heat these things together and pour over it; and serve it; garnish the Dish with boiled Onions and Barberries.

194. *To boil Pigeons with Capers and Samphire.*

Truss your Pigeons, and put them into a Pipkin with some Mutton broth and white Wine, a bundle of sweet herbs, when they are boiled, lay them into a Dish, then take some of the broth with some Capers and Limon sliced, and some butter, heat these together and pour over them; then fry thin slices of Bacon, and lay upon them, and some Samphire washed from the Salt, and some slices of Limon; Garnish your Dish with the same and serve it in.

195. *To boil Sausages.*

Take two pounds of Sausages, and boil them with a quart of Claret Wine and a bundle of sweet herbs, and whole Cloves and Mace; then put in a little Butter, when they are enough, serve them in with this Liquor and some Mustard in Sawcers.

196. *To boil Goose Giblets.*

Boil them with water and salt, and a bundle of sweet herbs, Onions and whole spice, when they are enough, put in Verjuice and Butter, and some Currans plumped, and serve them upon Sippets.

Thus you may dress Swans Giblets.

197. *To boil Giblets with Roots and good Herbs.*

Boil them in a quart of Claret, Ginger and Cloves, and a Faggot of sweet herbs, Turneps and Carots sliced, with good store of Spinage and a little salt; when they are enough, serve them upon Sippets.

And add to the Broth some Verjuice and the yolks of Eggs; Garnish your Dish with Parsley and pickled Barberries.

198. *To smoor a Neck of Mutton.*

Cut your Steaks, and put them into a Dish with some Butter, then take a Faggot of sweet herbs and some gross Pepper and a little Salt, and put them to them; cover your Dish, and let them stew till they are enough, turning them sometimes, then put in a little Claret Wine and Anchovies, and serve them upon Sippets.

199. *To smoor Veal.*

Cut thin slices of Veal and hack them over with the back of a Knife, then lard them with Lard, and Fry them with strong Beer or Ale till they be enough, then stew them in Claret wine with some whole Spice and Butter and a little salt.

Garnish your Dish with Sausages fryed; and with Barberries, to serve them in.

200. *To smoor Steaks of Mutton another way.*

Cut part of a Leg of Mutton into steaks, and fry it in White Wine and a little salt, a bundle of herbs, and a little Limon Pill, then put it into a Pipkin with some sliced Limon, without the Rind, and some of the Liquor it was fried in, and Butter and a little Parslie, boil all together till you see it be enough, then serve it in, and garnish your Dish with Limon and Barberries.

201. *To smoor Chickens.*

Cut them in Joints and fry them with sweet Butter, then take white Wine, Parsley and Onions chopp'd small, whole Mace and a little gross Pepper, a little Sugar, Verjuice and Butter, let these and your fried Chicken boil together, then fry the Leaves of Clary with Eggs, put in a little Salt to your

Chickens, and when they are enough, serve them in this fried Clary, and garnish your Dish with Barberries.

202. *To fry Museles, or Oysters, or Cockles to serve in with Meat, or by themselves.*

Take any of these and parboil them in their own Liquor, then dry them, flower them, and fry them, then put them into a Pipkin with Claret wine, whole Spice and Anchovies, and a little butter, so let them stew together, and serve them in either with a Duck, or by themselves, as you like best.

204. [Transcriber's note: so numbered in original] *To dress Calves feet.*

Take Calves feet tenderly boiled, and slit them in the middle, then put them in a Dish with sweet Butter, Parsley and Onions chopped a little Thyme, large Mace, Pepper with a little Wine Vinegar, and a little salt, let all these stew together till they are enough, then lay your Calves feet in a Dish, and pour the Sauce over them, then strew some raw Parsley and hard Eggs chopped together over them with slices of Limon and Barberries.

205. *To hash Neats tongues.*

Boil them and blanch them, and slice them thin then take Raisins of the Sun, large Mace, Dates sliced thin, a few blanched Almonds and Claret wine with a little salt; boil all these together with some sweet butter, verjuice and sugar; when they are enough, serve them in and thicken the Sauce with yolks of Eggs; garnish your Dish with Barberries.

206. *Another way to hash Neats Tongues.*

Boil Neats Tongues very tender, peel them and slice them thin, then take strong meat broth, blanched Chesnuts, a Faggot of sweet herbs, large Mace, and Endive, a little Pepper and whole Cloves and a little Salt; boil all these together with some butter till they be enough; garnish your Dish as before.

207. *To boil Chickens in white-broth.*

Take three Chickens and truss them, then take two or three blades of Mace, as many quartered Dates, four or five Lumps of Marrow, a little Salt and a little Sugar, the yolks of three hard Eggs, and a quarter of a Pint of Sack, first boil your Chickins in Mutton broth, and then add these things to them, and let them boil till they are enough, then lay your Chickens in a Dish, and strain some Almonds blanched and beaten into it, serve it upon Sippets of French Bread; garnish your Dish with hard Eggs and Limons.

208. *To boil Partridges.*

Put two or three Partridges into a Pipkin with as much water as will cover them, then put in three or four blades of Mace, one Nutmeg quartered, five or six Cloves, a piece of sweet Butter, two or three Toasts of Manchet toasted brown, soke them in Sack or Muskadine, and break them, and put them into the Pipkin with the rest, and a little Salt, when they are enough, lay them in a Dish, and pour this Broth over them, then garnish your Dish with hard Eggs and sliced Limon, and serve it in.

209. *To boil a Leg of Mutton.*

Take a large Leg of Mutton and stuff it well with Mutton Suet, Salt and Nutmeg, boil it in water and Salt, but not too much, then put some of that broth into another Pot, with three or four blades of Mace, some Currans and

Salt, boil them till half be consumed, then put in some sweet Butter, and some Capers and a Limon cut like Dice with the Rind on, a little Sack, and the yolks of two hard Eggs minced; then lay your Mutton into a Dish upon Sippets, and pour this Sauce over it; scrape Sugar on the sides of your Dish, and lay on slices of Limon and Barberries.

210. *To stew Trouts.*

Put two Trouts into a fair dish with some white Wine, sweet butter, and a little whole Mace, a little Parsley, Thyme and Savory minced, then put in an Anchovy and the yolks of hard Eggs; when your Fish is enough, serve it on Sippets, and pour this over it, and garnish your Dish with Limon and Barberries, and serve them in: you may add Capers to it if you please, and you may do other Fish in this manner.

211. *To boil Eels in Broth to serve with them.*

Flay and wash your Eels and cut them in pieces about a handful long, then put them into a pot with so much Water as will cover them, a little Pepper and Mace, sliced Onions, a little grated bread, and a little Yest, a good piece of sweet butter, some Parsley, Winter Savory and Thyme shred small; let them boil softly half an hour, and put in some Salt, with some Currans; when it is enough, put in Verjuice and more Butter, and so serve it; Garnish your Dish with Parsley, Limon and Barberries, put Sippets in your Dish.

212. *To boil a Pike with Oysters.*

Take a fair Pike and gut it and wash it, and truss it round with the tail in the mouth, then take white Wine, Water and Salt, with a bundle of sweet herbs, and whole Spice, a little Horse-radish; when it boils, tie up your Pike in a Cloth, and put it in, and let it boil till it swims, for then it is enough; then take the Rivet of the Pike, and a Pint of great Oysters with their Liquor, and some Vinegar, large Mace, gross Pepper, then lay your Pike in a Dish with Sippets, and then heat these just named things with some Butter and Anchovies, and pour over it; garnish your Dish as you please.

213. *To make a grand Sallad.*

Take a fair broad brimm'd dish, and in the middle of it lay some pickled Limon Pill, then lay round about it each sort by themselves, Olives, Capers, Broom Buds, Ash Keys, Purslane pickled, and French Beans pickled, and little Cucumbers pickled, and Barberries pickled, and Clove Gilliflowers, Cowslips, Currans, Figs, blanched Almonds and Raisins, Slices of Limon with Sugar on them, Dates stoned and sliced.

Garnish your Dish brims with Candied Orange, Limon and Citron Pill, and some Candied Eringo roots.

214. *To rost Pig with a Pudding in his Belly.*

Take a fat Pig and truss his head backward loking over his back, then make such Pudding as you like best, and fill his belly with it, your Pudding must be stiff, then sew it up, and rost your Pig, when it is almost enough, wring upon it the Juice of a Limon, and when you are ready to take it up, wash it over with yolks of Eggs, and before they can dry, dredge it with grated bread mixed with a little Nutmeg and Ginger, let your Sauce be Vinegar, Butter and Sugar, and the yolks of hard Eggs minced.

215. *To rost a Leg of Mutton with Oisters.*

Take a large Leg of Mutton and stuff it well with Mutton Sewet, with Pepper, Nutmeg Salt and Mace, then rost it and stick it with Cloves, when it is half rosted cut off some of the under side of the fleshy end, in little thin Bits, then take a Pint of Oisters and the Liquor of them, a little Mace, sweet Butter and Salt, put all these with the Bits of Mutton into a Pipkin till half be consumed; then Dish your Mutton and pour this Sauce over it, strew Salt about the Dish side and serve it in.

216. *To make a Steak-Pie.*

Cut a Neck of Mutton in steaks, then season it with Pepper and Salt, lay your Paste into your Baking Pan, and lay Butter in the bottom, then lay in your steaks, and a little large Mace, and cover it with Butter, so close it, and bake it; and against it is baked, have in readiness good store of boiled Parslie minced fine, and drained from the water, some white Wine and some Vinegar, sweet Butter and Sugar, cut open your Pie, and put in this Sauce, and shake it well, and serve it to the Table; it is not so good cold as hot.

217. *To rost a Haunch or a Shoulder of Venison, or a Chine of Mutton.*

Take either of these, and lard it with Lard, and stick it thick with Rosemary, then roft it with a quick fire, but do not lay it too near; baste it with sweet butter: then take half a Pint of Claret wine, a little beaten Cinamon and Ginger, and as much sugar as will sweeten it, five or six whole Cloves, a little grated bread, and when it is boiled enough, put in a little Sweet butter, a little Vinegar, and a very little Salt, when your meat is rosted, serve it in with Sauce, and strew salt about your Dish.

218. *To rost a Capon with Oysters and Chesnuts.*

Take some boiled Chesnuts, and take off their shells, and take as many parboil'd Oysters, then spit your Capon, and put these into the belly of it, with some sweet Butter, rost it and bast it with sweet Butter, save the Gravie, and some of the Chesnuts, and some of the Oysters, then add to them half a Pint of Claret Wine, and a pice of sweet Butter and a little Pepper, and a little Salt, stew these altogether till the Capon be ready, then serve them in with it; Garnish your Dish as you please.

219. *To rost Shoulder or Fillet of Veal with farcing herbs.*

Wash your meat and parboil it a little, then take Parsley, Winter-savory, and Thyme, of each a little minced small, put to them the yolks of three or four hard eggs minced, Nutmeg, Pepper and Currans and Salt, add also some Suet minced small; work all these with the yolk of a raw Egg, and stuff your Meat with it, but save some, and set it under the meat while it doth rost, when your meat is almost rosted enough, put to these in the Dish, a quarter of a pint of White Wine Vinegar, and some Sugar, when your meat is ready, serve it in with this Sauce, and strew on Salt.

220. *To make boiled Sallads.*

Boil some Carots very tender, and scrape them to pieces like the Pulp of an Apple, season them with Cinamon and Ginger and Sugar, put in Currans, a little Vinegar, and a piece of sweet Butter, stew these in a Dish, and when they begin to dry put in more Butter and a little Salt, so serve them to the Table, thus you may do Lettuce, or Spinage or Beets.

221. *To boil a Shoulder of Veal.*

Take a Shoulder of Veal and half boil it in Water and Salt, then slice off the most part of it, and save the Gravie; then take that sliced meat, and put it in a Pot with some of the Broth that boiled it, a little grated Bread, Oister Liquor, Vinegar, Bacon scalded and sliced thin, a Pound of Sausages out of their skins, and rolled in the yolks of Eggs, large Mace and Nutmeg, let these stew about one hour, than put in one Pint of Oisters, some sweet herbs, and a little Salt, stew them together, then take the bone of Veal and broil it and Dish it, then add to your Liquor a little Butter, and some minced Limon with the Rind, a Shelot or two sliced, and pour it over, then lay on it some fryed Oysters; Garnish your Dish with Barberries and sliced Limon, and serve it in.

222. *To boil a Neck of Mutton.*

Boil it in water and salt, then make sauce for it with Samphire and a little of the Broth, Verjuice, large Mace, Pepper and Onion, the yolks of hard Eggs minced, some sweet herbs and a little salt, let these boil together half an hour or more:

Then beat it up with Butter and Limon; then dish your Meat upon Sippets, and pour it on; garnish your Dish with the hard Whites of Eggs and Parsley minced together, with sliced Limon, so serve it; thus you may dress a Leg or a Brest of Mutton if you please.

223. *To stew a Loin of Mutton.*

Cut your meat in Steaks, and put it into so much water as will cover it, when it is scummed, put to three or four Onions sliced, with some Turneps, whole Cloves, and sliced Ginger, when it is half stewed, put in sliced Bacon and some sweet herbs minced small, some Vinegar and Salt, when it is ready, put in some Capers, then dish your Meat upon Sippets and serve it in, and garnish your Dish with Barberries and Limon.

224. *To boil a Haunch of Venison.*

Boil it in water and salt, with some Coleflowers and some whole spice; then take some of the Broth, a little Mace, and a Cows Udder boiled tender and sliced thin, a little Horse-radish root searced, and a few sweet herbs; boil all these together, and put in a little Salt, when your Venison is ready, dish it, and lay your Cows Udder and the Coleflowers over it, then beat up your Sauce, and pour over it; then garnish your Dish with Limon and Parsley and Barberries, and so serve it; this Sauce is also good with a powdered Goose boiled, but first larded.

225. *To make white Broth with Meat or without.*

Take a little Mutton broth, and as much of Sack, and boil it with whole Spice, sweet herbs, Dates sliced, Currans and a little Salt, when it is enough, or very near, strain in some blanched Almonds, then thicken it with the yolks of Eggs beaten, and sweeten it with Sugar, and so serve it in with thin slices of white Bread:

Garnish with stewed Prunes, and some plumped Raisins.

This may be served in also with any meat proper for to be served with white Broth.

226. *To make good stewed Broth.*

Take a hinder Leg of Beef and a pair of Marrow Bones, boil them in a great Pot with water and a little Salt, when it boiles, and is skimmed, put in some whole Spice, and some Raisins and Currans, then put in some Manchet sliced thin, and soaked in some of the Broth, when it is almost enough, put in some stewed Prunes, then Dish your Meat, and put into your Broth a little Saffron or red Saunders, some white Wine and Sugar, so pour it over your Meat, and serve it in; Garnish your Dish with Prunes, Raisins and fine Sugar.

227. *To stew Artichokes.*

Take the bottoms of Artichokes tenderly boiled, and cut them in Quarters, stew them with white Wine, whole Spice and Marrow, with a little Salt:

When they are enough, put in Sack and Sugar, and green Plumbs preserved, so serve them; garnish the Dish with Preserves.

228. *To stew Pippins.*

Take a pound of Pippins, pare them and core them, and cut them in quarters.

Then take a pint of water and a pound of fine Sugar, and make a Syrup, and scum it, then put in your Pippins and boil them up quick, and put in a little Orange or Limon Pill very thin; when they are very clear, and their Syrup almost wasted, put in the juice of Orange and Limon, and some Butter; so serve them in upon Sippets, and strew fine Sugar about the Dish sides.

229. *To make a Sallad with fresh Salmon.*

Your Salmon being boiled and souced, mince some of it small with Apples and Onyons, put thereto Oyl, Vinegar, and Pepper; so serve it to the

Table: Garnish your Dish with Limon and Capers.

230. *To rost a Shoulder of Mutton with Oisters.*

Take a large Shoulder of Mutton, and take sweet herbs chopped small, and mixed with beaten Eggs and a little Salt, take some great Oisters, and being dried from their Liquor, dip them in these Eggs, and fry them a little, then stuff your meat well with them, then save some of them for sauce, and rost your Mutton, and baste it with Claret Wine, Butter, and Salt, save the Gravie, and put it with the Oisters into a Dish to stew with some Anchovies, and Claret Wine: when your meat is enough, rub the Dish with a Shelot, and lay your meat in it, and then put some Capers into your Sauce, and pour over it, so serve it in; Garnish your Dish with Olives, Capers, and Samphire.

231. *To rost a Calves Head with Oisters.*

Split your Calves Head as to boil, and let it lie in water a while, then wash it well, and cut out the Tongue, then boil your Head a little, also the Tongue and Brains, then mince the Brains and Tongue with a little Sage, Oisters and Marrow put amongst it when it is minced, three or four Eggs well beaten, Ginger, Pepper, Nutmeg, Grated Bread and Salt, and a little Sack, make it pretty thick, then take the Head and fill it with this, and bind it close, and spit it and rost it, and save the Gravie which comes from it in a Dish, baste it well with Butter, put to this Gravie some Oisters, and some sweet Herbs minced fine, a little white Wine, and a sliced Nutmeg; when the Head is rosted, set the Dish of Sauce upon hot Coals with some Butter and a little salt, and the Juice of an Orange, beat it up thick and Dish your Head, and serve it in with this Sauce; garnish your Dish with stewed Oisters and Barberries.

232. *Sauce for Woodcocks Snites.*

When you spit your Fowl, put in an Onion in the Belly, when it is rosted, take the Gravie of it, and some Claret Wine, and an Anchovie with a little Pepper and Salt, so serve them.

233. *To make Sauce for Partridges.*

Take grated Bread, Water and Salt, and a whole Onion boiled together, when it is well boiled, take out the Onion, and put in minced Limon, and a piece of Butter, and serve them in with it.

234. *To rost Larks with Bacon.*

When your Larks are pull'd and drawn, wash them and spit them with a thin slice of Bacon and a Sage Leaf between the Legs of every one, make your Sauce with the Juice of Oranges and a little Claret Wine, and some Butter, warm them together, and serve them up with it.

235. *To make Sauce for Quails.*

Take some Vine Leaves dried before the fire in a dish and mince them, then put some Claret Wine and a little Pepper and Salt to it, and a piece of Butter, and serve them with it.

This Sauce is also for rosted Pigeons.

236. *To rost a whole Pig without the Skin, with a Pudding in his Belly.*

Make ready the Pig for the Spit, then spit it and lay it down to the fire, and when you can take off the Skin, take it from the fire and flay it, then put such a Pudding as you love into the Belly of it, then sew it up, and stick it with Thyme and Limon Pill, and lay it down again, and rost it and bast it with Butter, and set a Dish under it to catch the Gravie, into which put a little sliced Nutmeg, and a little Vinegar, and a little Limon and some Butter; heat them together: when your Pig is enough, bread it, but first froth it up with Butter and a little Salt, then serve it in with this Sauce to the Table with the Head on.

237. *To fry Artichokes.*

Take the bottoms of Artichokes tenderly boiled, and dip them in beaten Eggs and a little Salt, and fry them with a little Mace shred among the Eggs; then take Verjuice, Butter and Sugar, and the Juice of an Orange, Dish your Artichokes, and lay on Marrow fried in Eggs to keep it whole, then lay your Sauce, or rather pour it on, and serve them in.

238. *To make Toasts of Veal.*

Take a rosted Kidney of Veal, cold and minced small, put to it grated bread, Nutmeg, Currans, Sugar and Salt, with some Almonds blanched and beaten with Rosewater, mingle all these together with beaten Eggs and a little Cream, then cut thin slices of white Bread, and lay this Compound between two of them, and so fry them, and strew Sugar on them, and serve them in.

239. *To make good Pancakes.*

Take twenty Eggs with half the Whites, and beat them well and mix them with fine flower and beaten Spice, a little Salt, Sack, Ale, and a little Yeste, do not make your Batter too thin, then beat it well, and let it stand a little while to rise, then fry them with sweet Lard or with Butter, and serve them in with the Juice of Orange and Sugar.

240. *To fry Veal.*

Cut part of a Leg of Veal into thin slices, and hack them with the back of a Knife, then season them with beaten Spice and Salt, and lard them well with Hogs Lard, then chop some sweet herbs, and beat some Eggs and mix together and dip them therein, and fry them in Butter, then stew them with a little white Wine and some Anchovies a little while, then put in some Butter, and shake them well, and serve them in with sliced Limon over them.

241. *To make good Paste.*

Take to a peck of fine flower three pound of butter, and three Eggs, and a little cold Cream, and work it well together, but do not break your Butter too small, and it will be very fine Crust, either to bake meat in, or fruit, or what else you please.

It is also a very fine Dumplin, if you make it into good big Rolls, and boil them and butter them, or roul some of it out thin, and put a great Apple therein, and boil and butter them, with Rosewater, Butter and Sugar.

242. *To make good Paste to raise.*

Take to a Peck of Flower two pounds of Butter and a little tried Suet, let them boil with a little Water or Milk, then put two Eggs into your Flower, and mix them well together, then make a hole in the middle of your Flower, and put in the top of your boiling Liquor, and so much of the rest as will make it in to a stiff Paste, then lay it into a warm Cloth to rise.

243. *Paste for cold Baked meats.*

Take to every Peck of Flower one pound of Butter or a little more, with hot Liquor as the other, and put a little dissolved Isinglass in it, because such things require strength; you may not forget Salt in all your Pastes, and work these Pastes made with hot Liquor much more than the other.

244. *To make a Veal Pie in Summer.*

Take thin slices of a Fillet of Veal, then having your Pie ready and Butter in it, lay in your Veal seasoned with a little Nutmeg and Salt so cover it with Butter, and close it and bake it, then against it be drawn, scald some Goosberries or Grapes in Sugar and water as to preserve, and when you open your Pie, put in pieces of Marrow boiled in white Wine with a little blade of Mace:

Then put these Grapes or Goosberries over all, or else some hard Lettuce or Spinage boiled and buttered.

245. *To make a Pie of Shrimps, or of Prawns.*

Pick them clean from their Shells, and have in readiness your Pie with Butter in the bottom, then lay in your Fish with some large Mace and Nutmeg, and then Butter again, and so bake it:

Then cut it up and put in some White Wine and an Anchovy or two, and some Butter, and so serve them in hot; thus you may do with Lobsters or Crabs, or with Crafish.

246. *To make a Pie of Larks, or of Sparrows.*

Pluck your Birds and draw them, then fill the Bellies of them with this mixture following, grated bread, sweet herbs minced small, Beef Suet or Marrow minced, Almonds blanched and beated with Rosewater, a little Cream; beaten Spice, and a little Salt, some Eggs and some Currans, mix these together, and do as I have said, then having your Pie ready raised or laid in your baking-pan, put in Butter, and then fill it with Birds.

Then put in Nutmeg, Pepper and Salt, and put in the yolks of hard Eggs, and some sweet herbs minced, then lay in pieces of Marrow, and cover it with Butter, and so close it and bake it; then cut it open and wring in the Juice of an Orange and some Butter, and serve it.

247. *To make a Lettuce Pie.*

Take your Cabbage Lettuce and cut them in halves, wash them and boil them in water and salt very green, then drain them from the water, so having your Pie in readiness, put in Butter; then put in your boiled Lettuce, with some Marrow, Raisins of the Sun stoned, Dates stoned and sliced thin, with some large Mace, and Nutmeg sliced, then put in more Butter, close it and bake it; then cut it open, and put in Verjuice, Butter and Sugar, and so serve it.

[Transcriber's note: no number in original] *To stew a Neck of Mutton.*

Put your Neck of Mutton cut in Steaks into so much Wine and Water as will cover it, with some whole Spice, let it stew till it be enough, then put in two Anchovies, and a handful of Capers, with a piece of sweet Butter shake it very well, and serve it upon Sippets.

248. *To make a Pie of a rosted Kidney of Veal.*

Mince the Kidney with the Fat, and put to it some sweet herbs minced very small, a quarter of a pound of Dates stoned, and sliced thin and minced, season it with beaten Spice, Sugar and Salt, put in half a pound of Currans, and some grated bread, mingle all these together very well with Verjuice and Eggs, and make them into Balls, so put some Butter into your Pie, and then these Balls, then more Butter, so close it and bake it;

Then cut it open, and put in Verjuice, Butter and Sugar made green with the Juice of some Spinage, add to it the yolks of Eggs.

249. *To make a Potato Pie.*

Having your Pie ready, lay in Butter, and then your Potatoes boiled very tender, then some whole Spice and Marrow, Dates and the yolks of hard Eggs blanched Almonds, and Pistacho Nuts, the Candied Pills of Citron, Orange and Limon, put in more Butter close it and bake it, then cut it open, and put in Wine, Sugar, the yolks of Eggs and Butter.

250. *To make a Pig Pie.*

Spit a whole Pigg and rost it till it will flay, then take it off the Spit, and take off the Skin, and lard it with Hogs Lard; season it with Pepper, Salt, Nutmeg and Sage, then lay it into your Pie upon some

Butter, then lay on some large Mace, and some more Butter, and close it and bake it: It is either good hot or cold.

251. *To make a Carp Pie.*

Take a large Carp and scale him, gut and wash him clean, and dry him well, then lay Butter into your Pie, and fill your Carps belly with this Pudding; grated bread, sweet herbs, and a little Bacon minced small, the yolks of hard Eggs and an Anchovie minced, also a little Marrow, Nutmeg, and then put in a little Salt, but a very little, and make some of this up in Balls, then Lard the Carp, sew up his Belly, and lay him into your Pie, then lay in the Balls of Pudding, with some Oysters, Shrimps and Capers, and the yolks of hard Eggs and a little Slices of Bacon, then put in large Mace and Butter, so close it and bake it, then cut off the Lid, and stick it full of pretty Conceits made in Paste, and serve it in hot.

252. *To make an Almond Tart.*

Take a Quart of Cream, and when it boils, put in half a pound of sweet Almonds blanched and beaten with Rosewater, boil them together till it be thick, always stirring it for fear it burn, then when it is cold, put in a little raw Cream, the yolks of twelve Eggs, and some beaten Spice, some Candied Citron Pill and Eringo Roots sliced, with as much fine Sugar as will sweeten it, then fill your Tart and bake it, and stick it with Almonds blanched, and some Citron Pill, and strew on some small French Comfits of several colours, and garnish your Dish with Almonds blanched, and preserved Barberries.

253. *To make a dainty White-Pot.*

Take a Manchet cut like Lozenges, and scald it in some Cream, then put to it beaten Spice, Eggs, Sugar and a little Salt, then put in Raisins, and Dates stoned, and some Marrow; do not bake it too much for fear it Whey, then strew on some fine Sugar and serve it in.

254. *To make a Red Deer Pie.*

Bone your Venison, and if it be a Side, then skin it, and beat it with an Iron Pestle but not too small, then lay it in Claret wine, and Vinegar, in some close thing two days and nights if it be Winter, else half so long, then drain it and dry it very well, and if lean, lard it with fat Bacon as big as your finger, season it very high with all manner of Spices and Salt, make your Pie with Rye Flower, round and very high, then lay store of Butter in the bottom and Bay Leaves, then lay in your Venison with more Bay leaves and Butter; so close it, and make a Tunnel in the middle, and bake it as long as you do great Loaves, when it is baked, fill it up with melted Butter, and so keep it two or three months, serve it in with the Lid off, and Bay Leaves about the Dish; eat it with mustard and sugar.

255. *To make a Pie of a Leg of Pork.*

Take a Leg of Pork well powdred and stuffed with all manner of good Herbs, and Pepper, and boil it very tender, then take off the Skin, and stick it with Cloves and Sage Leaves, then put it into your Pie with Butter top and bottom, close it and bake it, and eat it cold with Mustard and Sugar.

256. *To make a Lamprey Pie.*

Take your Lamprey and gut him, and take away the black string in the back, wash him very well, and dry him, and season him with Nutmeg, Pepper and Salt, then lay him into your Pie in pieces with Butter in the bottom, and some Shelots and Bay Leaves and more Butter, so close it and bake it, and fill it up with melted Butter, and keep it cold, and serve it in with some Mustard and Sugar.

257. *To make a Salmon Pie.*

Take a Joll of Salmon raw, and scale it and lay it into your Pie upon Butter and Bay leaves, then season it with whole spice and a little Salt, then lay on some Shrimps and Oysters with some Anchovies, then more Spice and Butter, so close the lid and bake it, but first put in some White Wine, serve it hot, then if it wants, put in more Wine and Butter.

258. *To make a Pudding of French Barley.*

Take French Barley tenderly boiled, then take to one Pint of Barley half a Manchet grated, and four Ounces of sweet Almonds blanched and beeten with Rosewater, half a Pint of Cream, and eight Eggs with half the Whites, season it with Nutmeg, Mace, Sugar and Salt, then put in some Fruit, both Raisins and Currans, and some Marrow, mingle these well together, and fill Hogs Guts with it.

259. *To make a hasty Pudding in a Bag or Cloth.*

Boil a Quart of thick Cream with six spoonfuls of fine Flower, then season it with Nutmeg and Salt, then wet a Cloth, and flower it and butter it, then boil it, and butter it, and serve it in.

260. *To make a Shaking Pudding.*

Take a Quart of Cream and boil it, then put in some Almonds blanched and beaten, when it is boiled and almost cold, put in eight Eggs, and half the Whites, with a little grated Bread, Spice and Sugar, and a very little Salt;

Then wet Flower and Butter, and put it in a Cloth and boil it, but not too much, serve it in with Rosewater, Butter and Sugar, and strew it with small French Comfits.

261. *To make a Haggus Pudding.*

Take a Calves Chaldron well scowred, boiled, and the Kernels taken out, mince it small, then take four or five Eggs, and half the Whites, some thick Cream, grated bread, Rosewater and Sugar, and a little Salt, Currans and Spice, and some sweet herbs chopped small, then put in some Marrow or Suet finely shred, so fill the Guts, and boil them.

262. *To make an Oatmeal Pudding.*

Take the biggest Oatmeal and steep it in warm Cream one night, then put in some sweet herbs minced small, the yolks of Eggs, Sugar, Spice, Rosewater and a little Salt, with some Marrow, then Butter a Cloth, and boil it well, and serve it in with Rosewater, Butter and Sugar.

263. *To make Puddings of Wine.*

Slice two Manchets into a Pint of White Wine, and let your Wine be first mulled with Spice, and with Limon Pill, then put to it ten Eggs well beaten with Rosewater, some Sugar and a little Salt, with some Marrow and Dates, so bake it a very little, strew Sugar on it, and serve it; instead of Manchet you may use Naples Bisket, which is better.

264. *To make Puddings with Hogs Lights.*

Parboil them very well, and mince them small with Suet of a Hog, then mix it with bread grated, and some Cream and Eggs, Nutmeg, Rosewater, Sugar and a little Salt, with some Currans, mingle them well together, and fill the Guts and boil them.

265. *To make Stone Cream.*

Boil a quart of Cream with whole spice then pour it out into a Dish, but let it be one quarter consumed in the boiling, then stir it till it be almost cold, then put some Runnet into it as for a Cheese, and stir it well together, and colour it with a little Saffron, serve it in with Sack and Sugar.

266. *To make a Posset Pie with Apples.*

Take the Pulp of rosted Apples and beat it well with Sugar and Rosewater to make it very sweet, then mix it with sweet Cream, and the yolks of raw Eggs, some Spice and Sack, then having your Paste ready in your Bake-pan, put in this stuff and bake it a little, then stick it with Candied Pills, and so serve it in cold.

267. *To dry Pippins about* Christmas *or before.*

When your Houshold Bread is drawn, then set in a Dish full of Pippins, and about six hours after take them out and lay them in several Dishes one by one, and flat them with your hands a little, so do twice a day, and still set them into a warm Oven every time till they are dry enough; then lay them into Boxes with Papers between every Lay.

268. *To make Snow Cream.*

Take a Quart of Cream, and 4 Ounces of blanched Almonds, beaten and strained, with half a Pint of White Wine, a piece of Orange Pill and a Nutmeg sliced, and three Sprigs of Rosemary, mix these things together, and let them stand three hours, then strain it, and put the thick part into a deep Dish, and sweeten it with Sugar, then beat some Cream with the Whites of Eggs till it be a thick Froth, and cast the Froth over it to a good thickness.

269. *To boil Whitings or Flounders.*

Boil some White Wine, Water, and Salt, with some sweet Herbs and whole Spice; when it boils put in a little Vinegar, for that will make Fish crisp, then let it boil apace and put in your Fish, and boil them till they swim, then take them out and drain them, and make Sauce for them with some of the Liquor and an Anchovie or two, some Butter and some Capers, heat them over the Fire, and beat it up thick and pour it over them; garnish your Dish with Capers and Parsley, Oranges and Limons and let it be very hot when you serve it in.

270. *To make a Pie of a Gammon of Bacon.*

Take a *Westphalia* Gammon, and boil it tender with hay in the Kettle, then take off the Skin and stick it with Cloves and strew it with Pepper, then make your Pie ready, and put it therein with Butter at the bottom, then cover your Bacon with Oysters, parboiled in Wine and their own Liquor, and put in Balls made of Sausage meat, then put in the Liquor of the parboiled Oysters, some whole Spice and Bay Leaves, with some Butter, so close it, and bake it and eat it cold, you may put into it the yolks of hard Eggs if you please, serve it with Mustard Sugar and Bay Leaves.

271. *To bake a Bulloks Cheek to be eaten hot.*

Take your Cheek and stuff it very well with Parsley and sweet herbs chopped, then put it into a Pot with some Claret wine and a little strong Beer, and some whole Spice, and so season it well with Salt to your taste, and cover your Pot and bake it, then take it out, and pull out the Bones, and serve it upon tosted bread with some of the Liquor.

272. *To bake a Bullocks Cheek to eat cold, as Venison.*

Take a Bullocks Cheek, or rather two fair fat Cheeks, and lay them in water one night, then take out every bone, and stuff it very well with all manner of Spice and Salt, then put it into a Pot, one Cheek clapped close together upon the other, then lay it over with Bay Leaves, and put in a Quart of Claret Wine, so cover the Pot and bake it with Houshold Bread, when you draw it, pour all the Liquor out, and take only the fat of it and some melted Butter, and pour in again, serve it cold with Mustard and Sugar, and dress it with Bay Leaves, it will eat like Venison.

273. *To make a Bacon Froize.*

Take eight Eggs well beaten, and a little Cream, and a little Flower, and beat them well together to be like other Batter, then fry very thin slices of Bacon, and pour some of this over, then fry it, and turn the other side, and pour more upon that, so fry it and serve it to the Table.

274. *To make fryed Nuts.*

Take Eggs, Flower, Spice and Cream, and make it into a Paste, then make it into round Balls and fry them, they must be as big as Walnuts, be sure to shake them well in the Pan and fry them brown, then roul some out thin, and cut them into several shapes, and fry them, so mix them together, and serve them in with Spice beaten and Sugar.

275. *To make a* Sussex *Pancake.*

Take only some very good Pie Paste made with hot Liquor, and roul it thin, and fry it with Butter, and serve it in with beaten spice and sugar as hot as you can.

276. *To make a Venison Pasty.*

Take a Peck of fine Flower, and three Pounds of fresh Butter, break your Butter into your Flower, and put in one Egg, and make it into a Past with so much cold cream as you think fit, but do not mould it too much, then roul it pretty thin and broad, almost square, then lay some Butter on the bottom, then season your Venison on the fleshy side with Pepper grosly beaten, and Salt mixed, then lay your Venison upon your butter with the seasoned side downward, and then cut the Venison over with your Knife quite cross the Pasty to let the Gravie come out the better in baking, then rub some seasoning in those Cuts, and do not lay any else because it will make it look ill-favoured and black, then put some paste rouled thin about the Meat to keep it in compass, and lay Butter on the top, then close it up and bake it very well, but you must trim it up with several Fancies made in the same Paste, and make also a Tunnel or Vent, and just when you are going to set it into the Oven, put in half a Pint of Clarret Wine, that will season your

Venison finely, and make it shall not look or taste greasie, thus you may bake Mutton if you please.

277. *To make a brave Tart of several Sweet Meats.*

Take some Puff-paste, and roule it very thin, and lay it in the bottom of your baking-pan, then lay in a Lay of preserved Rasberries, then some more Paste very thin to cover them, then some Currans preserved, and then a Sheet of Paste to cover them, then Cherries, and another Sheet to cover them, then any white Sweet-Meat, as Pippins, white Plumbs or Grapes, so lid it with Puff-paste, cut in some pretty Fancy to shew the Fruit, then bake it, and stick it full of Candied Pills, and serve it in cold.

278. *To make Ice and Snow.*

Take new Milk and some Cream and mix it together, and put it into a Dish, and set it together with Runnet as for a Cheese, and stir it together, when it is come, pour over it some Sack and Sugar, then take a Pint of Cream and a little Rosewater, and the Whites of three Eggs, and whip it to a froth with a Birchen Rod, then as the Froth arises, cast it upon your Cream which hath the Runnet in it, till it lies deep, then lay on Bunches of preserved Barberries here and there carelesly, and cast more Snow upon them, which will look exceeding well; then garnish your Dish being broad brim'd with all kind of Jellies in pretty-fancies, and several Colours.

279. *To make a Mutton Pie.*

Cut a Loin or Neck of Mutton in steaks, and season it with Pepper and Salt, and Nutmeg, then lay it in your Pie upon Butter; then fill up your

Pie with Apples sliced thin, and a few great Onions sliced thin, then put in more Butter, and close it and bake it, and serve it in hot.

280. *To poach Eggs the best way.*

Boil Vinegar and Water together with a few Cloves and Mace, when it boiles break in your Eggs, and turn them about gently with a Tin slice till the White be hard, then take them up, and pare away what is not handsom, and lay them on Sippets, and strew them over with plumped Currans, then take Verjuice, Butter and Sugar heat together, and pour over, and serve them in hot.

281. *A good Sallad in Winter.*

Take a good hard Cabbage, and with a sharp Knife shave it so thin as you may not discern what it is, then serve it with Oil and Vinegar.

282. *Another Sallad in Winter.*

Take Corn Sallad clean picked and also well washed, and clear from the water, put it into a Dish in some handsom form with some Horse Radish scraped, and some Oil and Vinegar.

283. *To make Sorrel Sopps for Green Geese or Chickens, or for a Sick Body to eat alone.*

Take a good quantity of French Sorrel clean picked, and stamp it in a Mortar, then strain it into a Dish, and set it over a Chafing dish of Coals, and put a little Vinegar to it, then when it is thick by wasting, wring in the

Juice of a Limon and sweeten it with Sugar, and put in a little grated bread and Nutmeg, then warm another Dish with thin slices of white bread, and put some butter to your Sorrel Liquor, and pour over them, serve them in with Slices of Limon and fine Sugar.

284. *To make Green Sauce for a powdred Leg of Pork, or for a Spring.*

Take a great quantity of French Sorrel, and pick out the Strings and wash it well, and drain it clean from the water, then stamp it in a Mortar till it be extream fine, then put in grated bread and beat it again, then a few Currans and the yolks of hard Eggs, and when it is beaten to a kind of Pap, put in a little Vinegar and Sugar into it; so serve it in upon a Plate with your Meat.

285. *To make* Vin de Molosso, *or Treacle Wine.*

Take fair Water and make it so strong with Molossoes, otherwise called Treacle, as that it will bear an Egg, then boil it with a Bag of all kinds of Spices, and a Branch or two of Rosemary, boil it and scum it, and put in some sweet herbs or flowers, according to the time of the year, boil it till a good part be consumed, and that it be very clear, then set it to cool in several things, and when it is almost cold, work it with yest, as you do Beer, the next day put it into the Vessel, and so soon as it hath done working stop it up close, and when it hath stood a fortnight, bottle it, this is a very wholesom Drink against any Infection, or for any that are troubled with the Ptisick.

286. *For a Consumption, an excellent Medicine.*

Take Shell Snails, and cast Salt upon them, and when you think they are cleansed well from their slime, wash them, and crack their Shells and take them off, then wash them in the distilled Water of Hysop, then put them into a Bag made of Canvas, with some white Sugar Candy beaten, and hang up the Bag, and let it drop as long as it will, which if you bruise the Snails before you hang them up, it is the better; this Liquor taken morning and evening a Spoonful at a time is very rare.

287. *A Suitable Dish for Lent.*

Take a large Dish with broad Brims, and in the middle put blanched Almonds round about them, Raisins of the Sun, and round them Figs, and beyond them all coloured Jellies, and on the Brims Fig-Cheese.

288. *To make a Rock in Sweet-Meats.*

First take a flat broad voiding Basket, then have in readiness a good thick Plum Cake, then cut your Cake fit to the bottom of the Basket, and cut a hole in the middle of it, that the foot of your Glass may go in, which must be a Fountain-Glass, let it be as high a one as you can get; put the foot of it in the hole of the Cake edgling that it may stand the faster, then tie the Cake fast with a Tape to the Basket, first cross one way and then another, then tie the foot of the Glass in that manner too, that it may stand steady, then cut some odd holes in your Cake carelesly, then take some Gum Dragon steeped in Rosewater, and mix it with some fine Sugar, not too thick, and with that you must fasten all your Rock together, in these holes which you cut in your Cake you must fasten some sort of Biskets, as Naples Biskets, and other common Bisket made long, and some ragged, and some coloured, that they may look like great ill-favoured, Stones, and some handsome, some long, some short, some bigger, and some lesser, as you know Nature doth afford, and some of one colour and some of another, let some stand upright and some aslannt, and some quite along, and fasten them all with your Gum, then put in some better Sweet-meats, as Mackeroons and Marchpanes, carelesly made as to the shape, and not put on the Rock in a set form, also some rough Almond Cakes made with the long slices of Almonds (as I have directed before;) so build it up in this manner, and fasten it with the Gum and Sugar, till it be very high, then in some places you must put whole Quinces Candied, both red and white, whole Orange Pills and Limon Pills Candied; dried Apricocks, Pears and Pippins Candied, whole Peaches Candied, then set up here and there great lumps of brown and white Sugar-candy upon the stick, which much resembles some clusters of fine Stones growing on a Rock; for Sand which lies sometimes among the little Stones, strew some brown Sugar; for Moss, take herbs of a Rock Candy; then you must make the likeness of Snakes and Snails and Worms, and of any venomous Creature you can think of; make them in Sugar Plate and colour them to their likeness, and put them in the holes that they may seem to lurk, and some Snails creeping one way and some other; then take all manner of Comfits, both rough and smooth, both great and small, and colour many of them, some of one colour and some of another, let some be white and some speckled, then when you have coloured them, and that they are dry, mix them together and throw them into the Clefts, but not too many in one place, for that will hide the shape of your work, then throw in some Chips of all sorts of Fruit Candied, as Orange, Limon, Citron, Quince, Pear, and Apples, for of all these you may make Chips; then all manner of dryed Plumbs, and Cherries, Cornelions dryed, Rasps and Currans; and in some places throw a few Prunelles, Pistacho Nuts, blanched Almonds, Pine Kernels, or any such like, and a pound of the great round perfumed Comfits; then take the lid off the top of the Glass and fill it with preserved Grapes, and fill another with some Harts-horn Jelly, place these two far from one another, and if you set some kind of Fowl, made in Marchpanes,

www.ingramcontent.com/pod-product-compliance
Lightning Source LLC
Chambersburg PA
CBHW081109080526
44587CB00021B/3513